CREATEASCENE

Everything You Need To Know About The Art Department.

BRUCE HILL

First Published in Great Britain in 2013 by Norken Hill Publishing
Bordon, Hampshire GU35 0UY.

To learn more about about the author and to order copies please visit:

www.createascene.co.uk

ISBN: 978-0-9575192-0-6

Book and cover design by Bruce Hill.

Printed and Distributed in the UK by Print Media Solutions, The Shop, Church Square, Shepperton, Middlesex TW17 9JY.

CONTENTS

CREATEASCENE

Everything You Need To Know About The Art Department.

By Bruce Hill. ©

About This Book.

Many people outside and often within the film industry are intrigued by the techniques used to create scenery, props and effects for our industry. The object of this book is to provide an insight into this very specialised area of the trade. Why it's all done in a certain way and more importantly 'how it's done' on a practical level. It shows all aspects of the art department from initial script, research and set design, through to the building and painting of scenery and props up to the filming and strike. It is written for those wishing to learn more and to pursue a possible career in the art department. This is a book of solutions, gained from years of experience in the industry that takes a detailed look at virtually every aspect of the art department.

The pinnacle of a production designer's career is surely to work on successful feature films. But in order to achieve this goal he or she generally begins on smaller, more manageable productions. It is here that knowledge is nurtured, experience gained, and many flourishing careers are established. Unlike many other publications which specialise in feature film productions this book concentrates on those early steps in career development, on location and in studios, working on short films, pop videos, corporate films and commercials.

About The Author.

Bruce Hill started working in the film industry in the early 1980's after studying at Kingston Art College. He was introduced to the industry at an early age by his father, Ken, a well known scenic artist. Bruce began by assisting his father with scenic artwork on films like 'Alien' and 'Time Bandits'.

He soon became one of the youngest Art Directors of TV commercials in the business. In the Pop Video era of the late '80s, their family studio became a central hub for designing, building and shooting some of the best known videos of the time. Including early 'Simple Minds' and 'Peter Gabriel' promos, as well as all-time greats such as Michael Jackson's 'Billy Jean' and Kate Bush's 'Cloudbuster'.

Bruce's flourishing career as designer and art director continued with work on many award-winning commercials, short films and promos both in the UK and around the world.

Whilst lecturing at local film schools, he was often asked if he had ever considered writing a book that could be useful to aspiring film students.

This is the result!

Working with numerous renowned directors, producers and production companies over a period of more than 30 years, Bruce Hill is in a unique position to collect and collate the information required to write this book.

INTRODUCTION

 Virtually every movie has an art department. A dedicated team of people by whom nearly anything can be created. Anything, that is, as long as it looks believable.

A very able 1st assistant director once said to me astutely, "It's just like playing with large toys isn't it, looks great fun until it all goes wrong!" There are many that underestimate the art dept. The ability of a competent team may make it all look easy, however this is often the result of many years of experience in their specialised fields.

The hours are long, usually first in and last out sweeping the studio floor. A manic few days building, painting and dressing are followed by a long and often stressful pre light. Then come the very long shoot days ending with a set strike.

However, there is a certain satisfaction in achieving a seemingly impossible task in record time and seeing it being filmed. Can this be the reason we endure such punishment again and again? Pursuing greater and greater creative challenges.

Unlike many industries that work on longer time scales, the art dept turnaround on a short film or commercial is just a few concentrated days or weeks. Once all your

3

hard work is filmed and on celluloid or hard drive, the scenery is taken apart or thrown away. I maintain, as an art director of many years, that this strike can often be a cause for celebration, because, along with much of the scenery, many of the problems associated with the creation of the job are also disposed of.

Producers and directors often use the term 'hands on' when advertising for production designers and other members of the art department. This is correctly defined as;' Involving active participation, as opposed to theoretical'.

It is here where this book finds its target audience. As with any other trade, we will only succeed in actively participating, if we understand the mechanics of the medium we are working with. The materials and tools used in scenery and set design could be infinite. However, through the years we have refined this medium and the tools we use. As film scenery is temporary, compromises can be made (the important thing is to know where and when to compromise). This knowledge used to be passed down through the generations with apprenticeships. However, as the industry has expanded, apprenticeships have declined. The main source now for new entrants has become colleges, film schools and universities, hence the need for this book.

An art director should be a master of integration, who knows enough from the many learned trades and skills to be able to bring their disciplines together in a practical manner. This just so happens to be the exact definition of 'Jack of all trades, master of none'. However, to be successful, one needs to know when to delegate, and to contract a specialist, this point being better defined when one understands the medium one is working with.

It is not about creating the perfect designs, which is up to the individual. It is rather about which methods one should use to realise these designs, in a practical, cost effective and safe way.

THE FILM CREW

 A conception about a film crew is that there is a hierarchy from the producer and director down to the runner or stagehand, a little bit like a ship and it's crew. This is certainly true with regard to the wage scale and to a certain extent warranted. But one must consider how well a ship would sail with the captain alone; he needs his crew in order to go anywhere. Likewise a film cannot be shot without all involved and therefore respect should be allowed to everyone in that crew, not just the director.

Because films are inherently expensive to produce, a crew member not turning up or a poor looking set can let the whole production down, hence specialists are brought in for each and every task. An extra few hundred pounds spent in certain areas is such a comparatively small amount in the overall context and gives the producer security in knowing that each person will commit their best efforts and work long hours to assure a good result. It is for this reason that the professional crews are often paid more than their equivalent jobs in other trades, though this gap is becoming increasingly less. No two crews are the same but below is a typical list of the crew required to make a short film or commercial.

NON ART DEPARTMENT ROLES:

Production:

Producer: Oversees the whole production by securing the rights, agreeing the budget, hiring the director, key crew and talent.

Line Producer: This person would be in charge of overseeing the production budget, negotiating and hiring all the technicians or 'below the line' crew.

Production Manager: Responsible for organizing the facilities and day to day activities of the shoot, negotiating with crew and arranging immediate shoot requirements.

1st Assistant Director: Will liaise between production/crew and director reviewing takes and organizing positioning and timings of actors/sets.

2nd Assistant Director: Deals with background artists and generally assists the 1st assistant.

Location Manager: Will source locations and liaise with location owners. His team is also responsible for security and parking plus any permits required.

Camera:

Director of Photography or D O P: Responsible for the 'look' of the production, plus the camera and lighting kit. Also the choice of camera crew.

Camera operator: Operates camera or second camera if necessary (sometimes the D O P operates this).

Script Supervisor: Assists the director with script timings and continuity. Will take notes of good takes and frame numbers whilst filming.

Video Operator: Will record takes on separate video camera connected to the lens. This enables the immediate viewing of past takes.

Focus Puller: Helps set up the camera and changes lenses etc. Will take measurements prior to shots to create focus marks on the lens for use during tracking shots. Is ultimately responsible for the camera being in focus.

Camera Assistant/ Loader/ Clapperboard: This person loads the camera tape/ film /digital media and helps with the lenses plus logging shots and handling the clapperboard etc.

Camera driver: Stocks the camera truck and has thorough knowledge of what equipment is where on it. Keeps the truck accessible at all times.

Grip: Handles anything to which the camera is fixed, this could be anything from a specialist car rig, to legs or a camera dolly and tracks. Usually has his own truck.

First grip known as 'Key' followed by 'Second Grip' and 'Crane Technician'.

Lighting:

Gaffer: Works directly under the D O P selecting and booking crew and equipment. He positions lights and is usually placed near to camera delegating roles around the electrical department.

Sparks: The electrical department. Connecting and moving all lights and filters.

Genny Driver: Responsible for all remote power and position of generator plus associated kit.

Sound:

Sound Mixer: Will work (usually with a Boom operator) with his own equipment recording independent sound tracks throughout filming.

Costume, Wardrobe and Make-up:

Costume Designer: Will liaise directly with the Production Designer and Director to establish the 'look' of the clothes. Will usually have experience in the manufacture and design of clothes, sourcing and research. Will also create mood boards and budgets for the production.

Wardrobe Buyer: Will assist the designer sourcing, making and buying, plus taking care of outfits during the shoot.

Hair and Makeup: Specialist hairdresser and make up artist with own equipment standing by with all actors and cast.

7

Special Effects:

SFX Supervisor: Leads this department with thorough knowledge of all required effects.

Senior SFX Technician: Sets up/rigs all special effects with his team usually after preparations in his/her workshop.

SFX Technician: Acts as a second person to the above. Will usually have helped create the effects in a workshop prior to shoot.

The Art Department:

Slightly more detailed below are the main roles in the art and construction department. On small productions, where only one of each of the construction trade is required, his role is rated as 'master'.

Production Designer:

Liaising with the director, DOP and producer, the designer supervises the whole of the art department below. Being able to visualize the production and accurately budget the various departments plus calculate realistic time schedules. Essentially working with the director, visualizing the script and storyboard. Experience of the construction trades, research abilities, drawing and technical drawing skills. Most designers are also familiar with various postproduction, editing and lighting techniques.

Art Director:

Works on specific sets within the production dressing scenes and assuming position of designer in his/hers absence. Liaises directly with the designer, stylist and construction team-monitoring budget and time schedule. Able to draw and create technical drawings and make creative decisions on the designers behalf. Creates mood boards and sources special materials

Scenic Artist:

Working sometimes with an assistant, the scenic artist paints backcloths and scenery to help create specific locations or atmospheric conditions within the set. Capable of scaling up and replicating references onto large areas of a stage and familiar with all paints and spray techniques. Extensive knowledge of camera/ lighting/ viewing techniques is required to establish desired look of scenery plus realistic time scheduling. A scenic artist will carry his own, often specialist kit and reference material and be able to realistically create images according to the designer's brief.

Stylist/Set Decorator:
Creates the mood and feel, sourcing and budgeting the props. Works closely with the designer, visualizes and sources any special props required. Has an in depth knowledge of periods and styles, plus prop sourcing is a pre-requisite.

Buyer:
Working closely with the stylist sourcing, photographing, hiring, buying, and arranging pick-ups within the prop houses. Deals with all the necessary purchase orders and paperwork from production company and the suppliers. Arranges suitable transport and works on the logistics.

Master Prop man:
Responsible for all the props on set, unpacking and checking off etc. Works closely with camera crew on immediate details like dressing, moving props and arranging/ setting up pack shots. He will carry an extensive kit of tools, usually from his own van, He is capable of basic special effects and the set up of pack shots, labels and techniques for polishing, anti flare, smoke bubbles etc. He will be responsible for all continuity props and works/liaises directly with the art director, designer and stylist.

Props Assistant:
Assists the prop man and is familiar with the entire prop man's kit and layout. Will have experience checking off props and wrapping to avoid damage. Also aware of lifting, loading trucks and other techniques

Assistant Art Director:

Liaises with the art director on research and prop sourcing. Assists the prop man helping with dressing on all scenes. Sometimes responsible for the art department by standing in for the designer. Checks continuity and set dressing whilst filming. Takes care of dressing, striking and re dressing scenes.

Construction Manager:

Controls the set construction, liaising with the art director. He will order materials and book and pay all construction labour and transport plus arrange for the set strike. He works from the designer's drawings and with his own budget estimated by the Designer.

Rigger:

Riggers are responsible for erection and dismantling various rigs on a set from hung platforms through to basic towers. Also dealing with wire, fibre ropes, chains and slings, for hanging purposes. Rigger's must adhere strictly to relevant Health and Safety legislation and have the appropriate qualifications. There are various rigging grades such as: basic or advanced, electrical, standby, wire and stunt riggers.

Master Carpenter:

Takes care of all carpentry tasks such as building flats and other scenery specific items. Competent with reading construction drawings he is also skilled with film specific techniques such as weight and strength of various structures and finishes required for filming. A standby carpenter will also assist the grip in locking off camera rostra and moving/adjusting scenery when required.

Master Painter:

Paints all scenery and often primes backings for the scenic artist. Will liaise with the designer regarding any special finish, graining, ageing and marbling. He will also recommend preparation techniques and paint crew required. Will be able to assess quantities, types and colours involved to achieve desired finishes plus operate various spray guns and rollers.

Master Plasterer:

Works with all moulding in plasterwork and glass fibre, creating sheets of texture like brick and stonework, often joining/finishing sheets on set. Can create moulds of special surfaces for later replication. Usually carries various moulds for columns and balustrades made in a workshop.

Stagehand:

Works with the entire construction department, often stretching canvas for backings, operating scissor lifts/forklift trucks etc. (special license required) Moving parts of set on stage and generally tidying the stage during the build. He will assist the carpenters, painters and riggers during all stages of the build and will carry his own set of tools.

THE GREEN LIGHT

I'm going to assume here that a job has been confirmed and is already scripted and storyboarded. It is often at this stage where an art director is consulted.

Film is a visual medium and a storyboard, prior to filming, is by far the best method of communication. Don't let anyone tell you otherwise.

Storyboards:

A storyboard initially needs just to contain enough information to portray the idea of the film to others. So actors drawn as matchstick men are okay, provided people understand the drawings. The storyboard could be refined and updated as the job progresses prior to the shoot.

In my specific area, commercials, there are sometimes two storyboards. One beautifully drawn, specifically created to 'sell' the job to the client; this could normally be created by the ad agency or the production company and distributed amongst potential production companies in order to get various directors treatments and quotes. The second, being created by the director and storyboard artist, which, though often less finished, would be slightly more specific. It would generally contain timings of each frame and some more detailed shots.

There has only been one commercial I know of where the 'whole' crew got together as one, prior to filming, and talked through the job together. This was an English/ French/ Greek co production where good communication was imperative. Even on a thirty second commercial this can take considerable time - a valuable commodity in our industry. It is for this reason the storyboard is essential, so that even a runner, just brought in at the last minute, can get an immediate grasp of the job, saving valuable explanation time. If we take this one stage further, and put even more information on the board like say plan views showing where camera tracks could be laid, or action vehicles parked, then this info can be often used in the director's absence - a common situation on a dress or prep day (see following image).

Multi plate shots are becoming increasingly popular, where foreground action is filmed against a Chroma key backing and a separate 'plate' is filmed to use as a background image. It is essential for this to be made clear as the storyboard will only usually contain one frame instead of two, often-filmed on separate days. Each should take it's own place in the shooting schedule.

A storyboard can also be used simplistically to create a rough budget by assisting with a timing schedule. If one assumes each shot taking say half an hour to set up, 15 minutes to light and a further 15 minutes to shoot, some will be longer, some shorter. But on average each shot takes 60 minutes. Just count the pictures and you know how long it will take to film, a useful tip often overlooked.

To Summarise: The storyboard is a communication tool and can save considerable time on a shoot. The more information on the board, the more time saved, regardless of how good the drawings may be.

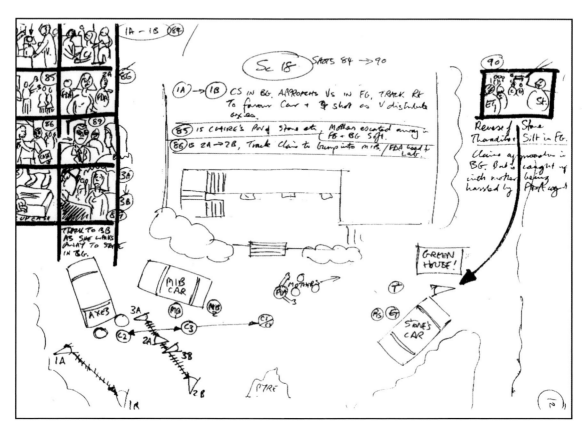

In the picture above, the director has drawn the positioning of all the action vehicles making the designer's and DOP's task a lot more straightforward in his absence, especially on prep days when things like generators and crew vehicles need parking up prior to shoot.

WHERE AN ART DIRECTOR STARTS

An art director/production designer starts very early in the production process, often only to assist the producer in the initial pricing up and quite often prior to the storyboard being drawn. It's useful to utilize the designers experience at an early stage as he/she might have tackled similar builds or unusual sets in the past and would be aware of any potential problems prior to final budget. It is perfectly feasible for a producer to contact a supplier direct in order to get an accurate cost but a designer will generally see a broader view and include logistical problems like specialist transport or setting up time. Something as simple as hiring a mobile crane can more than double in cost if one has it delivered and picked up out of hours or to an awkward location.

The usual career path of a production designer is through assisting established designers over a number of years, leading to controlling jobs in the designers' absence. This helps to build a personal track record, a good resume and eventually a show reel.

Initial Meetings:

Usually a meeting takes place to discuss primary issues prior to job confirmation. I must admit that I sometimes find these 'pre brief' meetings frustrating as we like to research our topics prior to discussing them, but there is a lot to be said for face-to-face contact. At these meetings, we often seem to be expected to know the costs of everything, from memory.

I much prefer to have a script/storyboard e-mailed, to have a telephone brief with the director and producer, do my research and then meet. I can then take in all appropriate references and costs and go away feeling that I have contributed somehow more. Also, a DOP is rarely about at this stage. Whenever they have been present I have found their contribution invaluable. The DOP is seeing the job from a different perspective and this is useful to all concerned. Is this a cost issue I wonder, because I've never charged for this part of the job, neither should they. The danger here is that we go to lots of meetings but gain no income if the job never happens. My own judgment would be, go for free, at least once, especially for a new client.

Research:

I have accumulated a large collection of reference books over the years and often leaf through them looking for ideas. However this can be time-consuming. The most commonly used method now must be the internet, especially initially. I do tend to find a lot of the internet material very Americanised though, which can be frustrating. As a result, should searches on the net fail, return to books. At this early stage it's worth creating a practical computer filing system within which all references can be easily accessed, I tend to name this file 'references'. This should accompany 'scripts/treatment' and 'budget' files. Within your 'refs' file should be all the arbitrary ideas, no matter how weird and wonderful. I try not to rename these in case the same website is needed later for more detailed research. So when the name is repeated, like 'Sienna', just adding a number '01' or '02' at the end of the existing file name keeps them in order.

I am surprised how often one refers back to this file later in the job when looking for small details, all so important to achieve realism. Printing out the total file in thumbnails can also be a great help when creating your initial designs with just a pad and pencil.

Visiting a real site to take reference photos is also useful but one can be easily influenced to the look of that particular site. At this early stage it's wise to remain more impartial to the more general ideas. It's also very time consuming so better left till your initial designs are completed.

You will find in the professional world that people want results almost instantaneously following the first meeting. So the successful designers role is often at the expense of the precious 'weekend off' for everyone else. Having said this a weekend 'drawing' can be very productive as one is not being phoned or mailed with urgent, often unimportant, messages from the production company thus allowing for absolute concentration at this critical 'ideas' stage.

Roughs:

For set sketches I would generally do about three pencil drawings of different ideas, using my references as a guide. It's a good idea to send these early on to the director, however rough they are, to get some initial thoughts and check that both of you are thinking around the same ideas. Hopefully one of these will spark some interest and this can then be refined later (see Drawings and Visuals later in this book). If one is fairly competent with perspective the initial sketches could potentially be scanned and coloured for your visual, or luckier still, be already sufficient for client presentation.

Preliminary Sketches sent unfinished for initial thoughts from the director.

It's quite common that within a brief there are some specific elements that require further research. I will now make initial calls to various companies to initiate a rough cost. Most suppliers need far more than just vague details so won't commit to any accurate prices but they might have an approximate idea and also highlight any potential problems.

Note: If that supplier is unable to help, "Do you know of anyone else?" is a good way to make each call productive.

Budgets are forever getting tighter and there is little point in completing designs that simply can't be afforded. Your sketches are useful here as they give an immediate idea of difficult areas so before going too far; doing a rough budget at this time gives an idea of potential costs.

A rough sketch of a hospital room set, with notes for discussion about the layout
The unusually tall walls are for a potential top shot.

A more refined sketch to enable initial research and budgeting.

The Recce:

All location jobs should have a recce. Just a small crew of location manager (responsible for the location search), DOP, director and producer will accompany the designer. We are usually offered a choice of suitable locations and I find a sat-nav essential when travelling between these (sometimes as much as ten in one day).

One can pre-programme all the locations for the day thus avoiding map reading, driving and possibly phoning simultaneously. As designers we have to consume vast amounts of information often knowing that many sites may be rejected for practical or visual reasons. There is rarely time to return that day so as well as providing your opinion, measuring and photographing needs to be done as quickly and efficiently as possible. As well as the script, storyboard and a notepad I would always recommend taking the following kit:

Digital camera: These come with remarkably high spec nowadays but I would recommend a camera with as wider lens as possible and actually filming on quite a low resolution. This saves time later when downloading and e-mailing to others.

Only when creating a photo-montage (for say a presentation) should one increase the image resolution. Bear in mind here that it is well worth trying to obtain some shots where you see the location alone, without people in them. Removing them later in photo-shop can be a laborious process.

Take as many photos as you can from every possible angle (not just where you are filming from). Another good tip is separating shots on your memory card by taking a shot of say 'your hand' between sequences. Each sequence then can be easily filed later to avoid confusion; this is especially helpful in places like supermarket aisles where many shots can look similar.

Colour Chart: Quite often we are asked to supply an extra wall or prop, to match an existing one at the location. With a colour chart, one can compare the colours with an existing wall giving us an exact reference for later colour mixing.

Tape Measure: For obvious reasons this is indispensable. However measuring is time consuming and the director and producer don't like hanging around. Quite often I will sketch a rough floor plan and measure just the really important bits (like ceiling height and access doors). The extra photos you have taken will give you most of the other information required. If you know the dimensions of say a standard door, and have a photo of the same door and a window, you can then calculate the size of the window by measuring the actual photograph later. Similarily, the size of a tiled floor can be calculated by measuring just one tile and counting the tiles in the photo. All very useful if your time is restricted.

Digital Tape Measure: Though I personally find these hard to trust they are useful for measuring points you can't physically reach such as high ceilings etc. Also, they are quick to use. Ceiling height is very important as it can make a big difference to the budget if using hired stock or specially built scenery.

Your opinions are vital during the recce. You should not just be looking at the proposed shot, whether it fits the brief, but also the logistics within each location like access and heights for your scenery or trucks. Tall buildings often have lifts, be sure to measure the door sizes.

Contact Sheet: Imperative if you're traveling independently and get lost.

Once final locations are selected get the owners/landlords contact details so you can arrange future lone visits should they be required, also if you need to deliver props early to site or need other information.

During the next week the Tech recce (for all heads of departments) should just be a formality. This is where you can confirm your measurements and say assist the grip by ordering more tracking boards etc. or helping with weather cover.

Finally, it can almost be guaranteed that whatever weather you get on a recce, the shoot will be the exact opposite!

CREWING UP AND BUDGETS

Crewing up:

Crewing up is a very individual process. A small job will require less crew making selection far more crucial. A good assistant is a very important choice, as you will spend a lot of often-stressful time with this individual and often have to delegate very diplomatic tasks. The same applies to your stylist. Although here it's often wise to choose someone who carries a certain in depth knowledge of the style of the job. Experienced stylists might be specialists in specific areas but should be familiar with most styles.

Both need to know how you work which makes it unwise to try out new people.

Hard as this sounds I tend only to risk new crew on the larger jobs where any misunderstandings are less crucial in the context of the overall job and can be corrected due to the longer time scale. Ironically, I find the best assistants are art directors in their own right, although on one occasion an assistant of mine completely changed in my absence assuming total control and clashing with my construction crew which was not desired, he didn't last long. This makes trust imperative.

I believe resourcefulness stands high, together with ability to take control of complete tasks from first phone call to delivery on site of specific items. This may sound simple, but when one is asked to get something, we designers don't want to know about all the logistics, especially if it's relatively trivial, we just want it there. Anticipation is another valuable asset, seeing a situation arise, and then solving it without the designer even knowing. These are assets which come with experience. Working away on another location knowing your stage build is being looked after well is very satisfying on any production.

Much of the above applies to choice of prop man but perhaps here attention to detail becomes paramount. Some of my best prop men have thoroughly analyzed the storyboard and schedule and pointed my attention (subtly) to any potential concerns and noticed small details that may easily have been overlooked. They have been 'sorters', as opposed to 'worriers', which is a big plus.

Choosing specialist subcontractors is more down to what they can do rather than to their characters. Our industry requires high standards in a very short space of time, quite often for a pre-arranged price. Pushing all the usual clients to one side to service one film job is challenging for any normal business outside of film and creates tension. We need to be aware of this and plan accordingly. I once had a whole case of plates requiring colour matched spraying, thrown to the ground, because I'd been phoning, checking and phoning again perhaps a little too often. This was a job that I'd like to erase from my mind. In retrospect it was probably down to my inexperience as opposed to the contractor's incompetence.

Crew Schedule:

A crew schedule is highly recommended when various locations are being shot on the same production. Everything is on a tight budget nowadays and it is wise for the designer to be one stage ahead, leaving the shoot, standby and strikes to assistants. I do find this extremely useful for lower budgets when some crew may be left without transport or tools in various locations. It is also a fantastic way to help create a budget by completing a schedule, as it soon identifies the minimum crew level required.

A good start here is to list all available crew, their contact numbers and whether they have transport. It's a good idea to have the same crew who initially prep a location, to be at that same location on the strike. This means that as they saw the site prior to shooting, they know how it should look at the end. This system is also worth following for the shoot standby, always ensure your key assistant is where the camera is, so there is continuity for the camera crew and they know who to relate to. If you have the luxury of a prop man, he would be by the camera. So broadly speaking for say 3 locations on a small shoot, 6 crew are required. Designer plus 1 on the advance build and dress, 2 by camera (one being the prop man), and 2 left tidying up and following on. This system is then rotated if you have say 5 locations so the person who was at the prep location goes on to strike it. It all sounds quite complicated but can be calculated easily on a spreadsheet, see the following image.

CLIENT DETAILS		NAME	CREW CONTACTS	E Mail	AREA CAR/NO CAR
For the attention of.	The Producer	KATE, Key Assistant	01234 5678910	key@assistant.com	Lewisham CAR
Production Company	As Above	MAX A, 2nd Assistant	01234 568976	Max@assistant.com	London W11 CAR
PRODUCT	JOB, No.	JOHN A, 3rd Assistant	0794 071 8035	JohnA@assistant.com	Near Tower Bridge CAR (rental)
Director	Jo Blogs	DAVID N, (New Guy)	07349 641 264	DavidNewGuy@mail.com	Leytonstone No Car
Tel. E mail		JONATHON W, (Work Experience)	07563 014 946	Jonathon@Experience.com	Ealing No Car
		IAN H, (Handyman)	07465625 817	ianhasvan@experience.com	Has VAN and tools

TIME	LOCATION/SET	DRESS AND BUILD	STANDBY	STRIKE AND PUT BACK	PERSONAL TRANSPORT
DAY 1					
					Kate to pick up David
6.30	FIELD	No Prep Required	Kate,John A,David N,Ian H	David, Ian	
11.30	BARN	John A, Ian H	Kate, John A	John A, David, Ian H	John to return David to tube
4.30	STREET SCENE PREP	Max A, All day (take food) Jonathon W, All Day			Max to pickup Jonathon (take lunch) Max to return Jonathon
DAY 2					
7.30	STREET SCENE	Prepped Day 1	Kate Max A. Jonathon W	Max A Jonathon W	Max to pick up Jonathon Max drive with Jonathon to new loc.
10.30	RUNNERS	John A, Ian H, David N	Kate, Ian, David	Ian, Max	John to pick up David
12.00	ROAD LOCATION	John A, Jonathon W	Kate, Max	Jonathon, Max	
4.00	VILLAGE HALL	John A, Ian H, David N (Max/Jonathon arrive later)	Kate, John A, Ian, Max	Ian, Max, Jonathon	Max to take Jonathon to nearest tube
DAY 3					
7.30	PARK SCENE	No Build Time	Kate, John A, David N	John A, David N	Kate to pick up David
12.00	RECREATION GROUND		Kate, (Max, Jonathon late call)		Jonathon to make his way to W11 to be picked up by Max
4.30	SUPERMARKET	John A, David N	Kate, Max, Jonathon (Kate leav	John A, David N (then wrap)	
6.00	REAR SUPERMARKET		Max, Jonathon	Max, Jonathon (then wrap)	Kate to take back whoever

A crew schedule above. Note how the same crew initially on the build/dress is also present for the wrap and tidy up. Also that the same person is attending the camera crew at all locations, this aids communication through the unit.

Budgets:

It will not be long before the producer gets in touch to ask how much. This leads me to a little gripe. If a job gets to a certain stage, the producer will have already done a rough budget. Why do they not just tell us how much they have allowed as opposed to letting us speculate whether our price is too expensive or too cheap? Perhaps they think that there is just a hope, that we might come in well under price and increase their profit margin as a result. If a designer wishes to work again he/she will not deliberately try to rip anyone off, it's self-defeating! We need the next job as well. In my broad opinion we spend far too much time addressing cost issues as opposed to design issues.

An experienced designer should have an idea how long it will take to build something and therefore to cost it out. Each has his own methods but I tend now to use a basic principle that say if you employ a carpenter for a whole day, there is a limit to the amount of materials he can use in that time. Once you have calculated how long it would take to make an item, you add a percentage on for materials. As the materials must include all the sundry items like tape, nails, screws and compressor hire, and, rather than calculate this, I just put on say 75% of the labour cost. I use a pre-formatted spreadsheet listing all the extra, often forgotten items like 'construction transport' and 'skip' for rubbish clearance. This is very useful as it acts as a reminder for all those things easily overlooked when being pushed for a price in restricted time. If one is using especially expensive materials, like glass or high gloss surfaces, one increases the percentage.

Other costs can also be quickly calculated on this spreadsheet such as 'National Insurance Tax' and 'Construction Company mark up'.

I try to keep the sheet down to one printable page so producers can see, at a glance, the overall figure of the art department, sometimes giving a separate props breakdown on another sheet, with just a total on page one.

Example:

Suppose one is doing a budget of say a small three-walled set with one door and two windows, and some basic dressing, including wall pictures a sofa and chair. If I were a set carpenter it would take a quarter a day to load a truck (night before), with a mate. Another half day to make up the window reveal/door fillers. A further half day to mark out, lay out the flattage, cover with canvas and stand up and brace the set. A painter could then put on the priming coat. Day 2 would be spent cutting mouldings, fitting windows, hanging door, painting and fitting flooring. This leaves day 3 for dress and light although, more realistically/usually we are asked to achieve this in 2 days overall (because of stage rental cost being expensive and priced daily) meaning some labour will be working overtime. Then we need to take the set out, so add 2 further crew for one day (this would include initial truck loading). So, for construction it will be 3 x crew for say two and a half days, now some of this is overtime, so effectively we have 3 days for 3 crew plus strike-out, total 11 man days.

Each Man Costs:

Man Daily rate = X (this amount varies per year according to local rates)

Construction Company Mark Up = 20%

Tax National Insurance = 12.8% (present UK rate)

Total Crew 11(X+20%+12.8%)

Total Materials = above cost (X) x 85%

Add Transport and waste disposal.

Other costs: You will need a stylist for prop selection, an assistant, some transport and of course, some props and possibly a prop man. I tend to price these individually as their cost can vary so much (sometimes an assistant will work for less as they get more days or need the experience). You also may require a standby carpenter, which can be negotiated separately. Finally of course, don't forget your own fee!

Pre-formatted spreadsheets can be created in excel as on the following page. Notice the grey tabs at the bottom can be used to provide more detailed breakdowns.

1	BRUCE HILL. PRODUCTION DESIGNER. TEL.NO					Date	04/11/2010
2	For the attention of.						
3	Production Company						
4	Production						
5	Tel/fax						
6	**Please Note: This is an Estimate, not a quotation.**						
7	CONSTRUCTION LABOUR		CHIPPY	PAINTER	RIGGER	STAGE H.	
8	DAYS		Crew	Crew	Crew	Crew	total crew of
9	Pre Build Days						0
10	Recommended Studio Build Days						0
11	Prelight Days	Day 1					0
12	Shoot Days	Day 2					0
13	Strike Days	Day 3					0
14		Strike					0
15							0
16			Total Man Days			Days	0
17			Skilled Crew Rate			Labour Tot	0.00
18	Construction Materials As A Percentage Of Labour			Rate	85.00	%materials	0.00
19	Construction Manager		Days	Rate			0.00
20					Construction Transport		
21						Skip	
22	Contruction Company Mark up.			Rate	20.00	%	0.00
23	National Insurance on Labour @12.8%			Rate	12.80	%	0.00
24	Total Construction					Total	0.00
25							
26	Metal/Plasterwork						0.00
27	Modelmaking						
28					Total Modelmaking	0.00	0.00
29	Scenic Artist	Or Photobacking		Days At		Per Day	0.00
30	Special Effects	Rain wind or smoke					
31					Total SFX	0.00	0.00
32	Props	Please Click Tab Below for Breakdown					
33					Total Props	0.00	0.00
34	Props Transport				Props Transport		0.00
35							
36	Props Stylist			Days At		Per Day	0.00
37		Car Parking expense	0	Days At		Per Day	0.00
38	Assistant Art Director			Days At		Per Day	0.00
39	Art Direction			Days At		Per Day	Total Fees	0.00
40							
41	Standby Construction on shoot	Crew		Days At	0	Per Day	0.00
42					Total Skilled Crew	0.00	0.00
43	Propman	Dress/Strike out	8Hrs		0	Per Day	0.00
44		Shoot	10Hrs		0	Per Day	0.00
45					Props Kit	per job	0.00
46							
47	TOTAL ART DEPT PRODUCTION>						0.00

Use these tabs

Overall / Props Estimate / Materials /

29

Budgeting for feature films:

Features are more complicated to budget and the script requires a thorough breakdown prior to pricing.

Following an initial read-through to get a grasp of the story each scene needs listing on a spreadsheet. This should list various items, useful for later like: Scene number, script page, night or day, location, length, what briefly happens and any specific items required. As one reads through the script and returns to the same locations, they should be inserted in the specified location on the spreadsheet. When complete the document will show a complete summary of how many locations, what sets are required plus those most frequently used. Plus of course details of props, effects and graphics needed for each scene. This leads to an accurate cost breakdown and you can refer back to it during the build and shoot.

Breaking down the script in this way, though time consuming, enables the designer to easily delegate certain scenes and to decide which deserves the largest budget allowance. It also gives the designer an instant reference when filming as to what's required for each scene.

Each set can then be individually priced for labour and materials with a separate area for the props and effects. Prop houses base their hire charges on replacement value, usually 10% for one week, 15% for two weeks and so on with further discounts available for longer periods of hire. A contingency should be allowed for sundry items and unscripted additions. Construction rates vary and could include working a six-day week and a 10 or 12-hour day so it's wise to be able to adjust the rate easily on a spreadsheet as a whole. The term 'man day' is useful placed somewhere high on the sheet to explain exactly how many hours a crewmember works and whether building or shooting. Another accurate way is to agree an 'hourly rate' instead of 'daily rate'. This hourly rate remains constant no matter how many hours are worked, below the legal maximum of course.

By law we are required to have rest breaks of at least 11hrs, weekly breaks of at least 35 hours or a fortnightly break of at least 59hrs.

Page	D/N	Scn	Loc	HowLong	Brief Description	Props/SFX	Graphics
	ART DEPT SCRIPT		Breakdown				
109	Dawn	162	Exterior Warehse	1/8	Petri stares at open gate and beyond. Morning sun, chainlink fence, pill bottle in hand	Pill bottle	
115	D	173	Ext Warehse Field	1/8	Petri Escapes through the field		
116	D	175	Ext Warehse Field	1/8	Petri running.		
116	D	177	Ext country Road	1/4	A vehicle approaches and Petri slumps on bonnet, Young couple in vehicle.		
117	D	178	Int Sports car	3/8	Petri in back, cars swoosh by going other way, Petri with pills. Just starts to go to sleep. END.	Action cars, Pills	
1	D	1	Interior Warehse E	1/8	Establishing Shots	Red Lights Flashing	
1a	D	3	Interior Warehse E	1/8	Establishing Shots	Red Lights Flashing	
29	D	38	Int Warehse	1/8	Black suits moving around inside DAY THREE' title.		
48	D	64	Int Warehse	1/8	Red Pulsating alarm lights on centre	Red Lights C/U	
53	N	73	Int Warehse	1/8	We descend on Testing Bay from above. 4 black shapes around table		
69	N	93	Int Warehse	1/8	Lights on complex are dimmed, during the night.		
76	N	107	Int Warehse	1/8	Complex seen in silhouhette.		
77	N	109	Int Warehse	1/4	Phil appears to be outside the room looking in. He sees Petri and Steve inside.		
80	N	113	Int Warehse	1/8	Shot from above we see subjects in factory room.		
115	Dawn	171	Int Warehse	1/8	We see Petri sprint towards warehouse door split (light shining through).		
2	D	11	Vault	3/4	2Way Mirror tiny CCTV Cameras Speakers fairly high up		
					Sliding Doorway with window at far end		cctv images
					Sliding entrance Hatch. Bright lights	Practical Shower heads	
3	D	13	Vault	1 1/4	Taking off clothes Containers for patients clothes	Steam, Water	
					Steam erupts from all angles	Showers/drain	
	D	12	Vault	1/8	Police observe from other side.	(plumber st by)	
4	D	14	Int House	1/2	Bottom of a Long tunnel. Several cubicles seperated by opaque dividers		
	D	5	Int House	1/8	Led further down tunnel		
37	D	52	Int House	1	Petri in cubicle under a flickering light. Grabs towel from locker nearby.		
	D	66	Int House	1/8	3 x Guards race through wheeling crash cart and medics		Name tags on suits
63	D	87	Int House	1/4	Mike bounces ball, he misses it and it goes down entrance tunnel	Towel	
	N	98	Int House	5/8	Mike gets frustrated as his reflexes aren't good (ball throwing).	Crash Cart/Guard.	
107	Dawn	154	Int House	1/8	Guards leave with 2 crash trolleys. Outer hatch seals behind them.		
112	Dawn	167	Int House	1/2	The two struggle down tunnel. Door, a dark figure the other side. It's Rick, no it's not.		
115	Dawn	169	Int House	1/8	Petri sprints towards open hatch.		
50	D	70	Int Factory	1/4	Dr Wise in corridor. Jane on Stretcher. Makeshift Cleanroom set up		
50	Dusk	71	Int Factory	1/2	Makeshift Ward. Curtain pulled around body. Dr wise gets taken away by guards.	Baseball	
58	N	80	Int Factory	7/8	Dr Wise tries to persuade Yun to re issue the drug and is turned away. Trouble reported from Guard.	Id tag	
107	Dawn	156	Int Factory	1/8	Doors open, trolley wheels through. Plastic freezers either side containing oitment.	Flight cases, trolley,	
88		119	Int Factory	1/8	Dr. Wise searches all doors until he finds the 'Server' Room.	Clipboards	Artwork for
91	N	128	Int Factory	1/8	Dr Yok strides through corridors flanked by Guards.		
97		135	Int Factory	1/8	A Guard tries door to server room, it's locked. Get it open now! (Yok)		
107	Dawn	157	Morgue	1/2	Guard disinfects hands. A mortician starts disecting Mike. Petri slides hidden between cases. She attacks Mortician.		Morgue, dispenser.
111	Dawn	165	Morgue	1/8	Guard realises that Petri body in bag has been replaced by Morticians. Pushes Alarm	Clipboard. Alarm button.	

A feature film script breakdown.

Another area often neglected is production expense. We are often asked to provide trestle tables and chairs or wardrobe rails and items never seen on camera. These should be listed separately from the art department budget as 'production expenses' and will often require their own designated transport. It is impossible to accurately forecast how much these may cost as the production office may have numerous unexpected requests, like fridges and microwaves for their office, or heaters/air conditioners etc..

Petty Cash:

Many of the smaller jobs involve dealing with cash rather than exhaustive budgeting and for obvious reasons you must try to avoid using your own funds. A cash float should always be available at the start of any production. If, for some practical reason, you are forced to pay for anything, it is wise to put these purchases on a separate credit card reserved for work transactions only.

For these an allowance must be made for VAT because your purchases will generally have this included. Be sure to keep all the receipts and check they are vat registered (there is usually a vat registration number on them). Some companies have their own vat forms for petty cash advances (disbursements) but these generally require filling in by hand and I find it a lot easier just to create my own form as the rate can be automatically calculated just requiring totals, dates and descriptions to be filled in. Bear in mind here that when the job is completed it's good practice to number your receipts and staple them in order to sheets of plain white paper, these sheets should then be sent to your client with a copy of your breakdown. This makes it easier for the company accountant as they are rarely near the shoot and don't know what's been spent or where. Make sure you have included the initial float given and whether you owe or are owed money after the job.

VAT should never be included in your final cost summary as your client will, or should, be claiming this element back and it will not tally with the producer's budget, which is usually net as opposed to gross.

All of the above can be calculated with an excel spreadsheet shown on the following page:

Remember also to keep your fee separate from any purchases made, as this should be on a separate invoice.

It's good practice to scan/photocopy all your receipts used on productions as some payments may have gone through your own bank account and you will have sent the originals to your client leaving no personal proof of purchase; this may affect your tax position.

BRUCE HILL   ART DIRECTOR   Petty Cash Expenses

For The Attention of				Date.	04/11/2010
Production				Sheet No.	
Job No.				Currency	Sterling
Shoot Dates					
Re Purchase order					

Ref	Date	Detail	EX VAT	VAT	TOTAL
1	04/06/2010		0.00	0.00	
2			0.00	0.00	
3			0.00	0.00	
4			0.00	0.00	
5			0.00	0.00	
6			0.00	0.00	
7			0.00	0.00	
8			0.00	0.00	
9			0.00	0.00	
10			0.00	0.00	
11			0.00	0.00	
12			0.00	0.00	
13			0.00	0.00	
14			0.00	0.00	
15			0.00	0.00	
16			0.00	0.00	
17			0.00	0.00	
18			0.00	0.00	
19			0.00	0.00	
20			0.00	0.00	
21			0.00	0.00	
22			0.00	0.00	
23			0.00	0.00	
24			0.00	0.00	
25			0.00	0.00	
26			0.00	0.00	
27			0.00	0.00	
28			0.00	0.00	
29			0.00	0.00	
30			0.00	0.00	

	TOTAL	0.00	0.00	0.00

FLOAT RECEIVED		
BALANCE		
TOTAL	You Owe Me	

Standard Petty Cash Form.

Budget Approval:

It's a rare thing to get instant approval and go-ahead on any job although I do find it gets a fairly quick response once the estimate is sent, somehow bringing a certain reality to the whole project in the producer's mind. One is never absolutely sure that the client hasn't been to numerous designers, and it's for this reason that overpricing in unwise. A reputation of being expensive is hard to lose. Under pricing also presents uncertainty without justification. I must admit that I sometimes delay in sending my estimate too early so I can think over it very carefully, ideally overnight prior to presenting it. It's amazing how many times one thinks of a better idea or alternative method of building after a good night's sleep, or remembers something vital, yet unquoted.

The common initial response I tend to get is; "That takes us over budget, are there any ways of reducing it?" or "We'd better have a re-think here". However, the knowledge that you have thought carefully about the budget and can justify all your figures tends to put it straight back into production's hands (i.e. write a cheaper script).

This brings me to another scenario where a client says they have say £8500.00 for the Art Department but that includes your fee. It may sound a lot but once you count your prep time, build time and shoot time, and especially the many evenings, the money goes quickly, so it's always wise to separate out your fee first.

It's quite common for a director to work for nothing on a job. But would you, as a designer, ask a carpenter for a few days work for nothing? So why should they ask you? It provides them with an addition to their show reel to progress their career. You will find generally that as you've made extraordinary efforts to please them, you've also made budget compromises and it is these that will be remembered, not your offer of your free time. This is where many inexperienced designers fail. We have overheads, like anyone else, and no matter how much "fun" the job may be described as, it is hard work, which carries considerable responsibility, and this needs reward.

Some of my most challenging jobs have been so-called 'freebies'. One uses up all one's crew favours, and, because the job is 'not as good as it could be', the clients, who eventually get good paying jobs; go elsewhere to pay for a better finished set.

So you have been warned, I'm not saying "don't do them", I'm saying, "treat them with extreme caution".

One other point on budgets; An 'estimate' is a professional's opinion as to how much a job will cost, whereas a 'quote' is a price for which one is happy to complete a job for. This can have legal connotations and because of the nature of our profession the brief is quite often not the same at the conception as it is at the shoot. So you would be well advised to provide the former, to prevent being tied to your price.

Sometimes a frustrating wait follows your budget submission and this to can be crucial. Your prices have been collated on the assumption that this can all be done in a realistic timescale, in order to keep to the existing schedule. The longer they wait, the less realistic this budget becomes as there is less time to build the set. It is sometimes wise to remind the producer that excessive delays in approval may lead to extra-incurred overtime, hence increasing the costs.

On one occasion I was only allowed to confirm enough labour and materials for just one day, out of a six-day build, whilst awaiting approval. This obviously disrupts all attempts to keep within budget as one can't keep key crew or get bulk discounts on materials.

DRAWING AND VISUALS

One must bear in mind here that a designer is 'just that' and we should not necessarily be expected to be able to draw and paint to an exceptionally high standard. It helps to be able to draw, and our skills should ideally be adequate to portray information to others but there is rarely enough time to complete masterpieces suitable for a gallery, in fact I know of many successful designers who claim to be incapable of drawing.

If drawing skills are below par there are many other ways of achieving a suitable design for clients and crew. For the un-initiated I would highly recommend doing a Photoshop course and possibly a few tutorials in Sketch-up. This could be time 'very well spent' to make your life easier in your future career.

Photo Montage:

Quite often we are required to mock up a location to show how a scene might look when finished. I often use one of my 'clean' location photos. Create new layers in photo-shop and simply draw or paste on top. This is where your initial location and reference photos become invaluable.

The following images show one of my initial location photos. The director was very specific about the design of a Santa's Grotto within, so this is first sketched, at a rough camera height, for approval, then rendered in colour against black (for easy selection, copying and pasting within Photoshop). A montage showing other selected references is then added to represent the Christmas fair. These reference stills are often resized, flipped or distorted in photo-shop so as to fit into the desired location photo. Once complete, the image can be 'flattened' to reduce file size, then sent to client. Keep the un-flattened version though, in case more editing is required, it's often more than the director, who needs satisfying.

Initial Recce Photo.

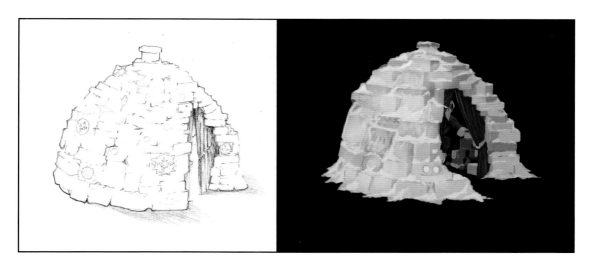

A sketch of a grotto scanned and rendered in Photoshop. Take care to match the direction of light in the recce photo when colouring. The black background was created to make selection of the grotto easier when pasting onto the location photo.

The completed photo montage. An ideal technique for those unsure about their drawing abilities.

Visuals:

Time is valuable, and much as I love the traditional mediums like watercolours, crayons or marker pen drawings I'm afraid they are now superseded by computer graphics in our industry. The one major advantage is that these are ultimately editable and e-mailable. Computer graphics can bring certain disadvantages, providing a near photo realistic result, if one is anal enough. It is sometimes wise to leave certain items like wall colours and floor surfaces 'vague' so one doesn't tie oneself down to specifics, but instead gives 'just an impression' with room for adjustment. At this stage all materials and props research is not yet complete and decisions haven't been finalised. One then can't be accused of not being able to produce a set like the visual. I find that visuals or concept sketches are often used to sell the job, and to impress the clients enough to allow final release of funds, important though that is. If one of those moneymen doesn't want that 'ornate chair' that took 2 hours for you to draw, you have to replace it. Worse still, if someone really likes that ornate chair and it's not available for your shoot! A looser design is often preferable; this can then be scanned for rendering in colour. Knowledge of perspective is an advantage but try to keep it simple, as it can be time consuming. There are various options to choose from regarding a finished visual.

A simple perspective sketch:

Coloured later by hand or rendered on computer. This is good for keeping your ideas flexible but can be time consuming later when scaling up accurately for the construction drawings. A sketch is useful if alternative ideas are required or just suggestions. Once the final sketch is agreed it can either be developed directly or re made in basic 3D (as on page 43). I sometimes recreate the basic shapes in the 3D model, then rotate the model to the desired viewpoint, print it out and trace over in pencil to add small details. I then re-scan and send to clients. This process is not only quick, but secure in that you know and can relate back to the 3D model for scaling and later development.

A 2D computer mock-up:

This can be good for those not proficient at drawing or 3D programs but can look clinical and lack emotion and atmosphere. Shapes created initially on computer are easy to create then rendered in colour. It's worthwhile incorporating as many photographic references here to enhance the overall look.

A 3D design:

This takes a lot longer to initiate but saves considerable time later in the process as all your initial work can be used for the scale drawings. The drawback here is the time to construct, as the job may not be confirmed and some items may take considerable effort to produce (often the simplest ones to draw by hand!). It's also worth remembering that this design will often just be seen in 2D, as it may be e-mailed to numerous people, so it does want to look fairly proficient. The time taken here can often be wasted, as your client may have radical new thoughts upon seeing it for the first time and ask for changes. This could mean a complete rebuild of the 3D model.

An initial 'Old school' pencil illustration is often the best place to start. Light is important in the shading to increase the atmosphere and give the design realism.

Once sketch is scanned it can be rendered in Photoshop with final lighting effects applied on a separate layer.

If one creates a 3D plan in Sketch-up it can be exported as 2D into Photoshop for rendering, however one can also change the styles whilst still in Sketch-up so exporting three styles to use as separate layers can be very useful for all the selection tools in Photoshop (see next image) making rendering considerably quicker.

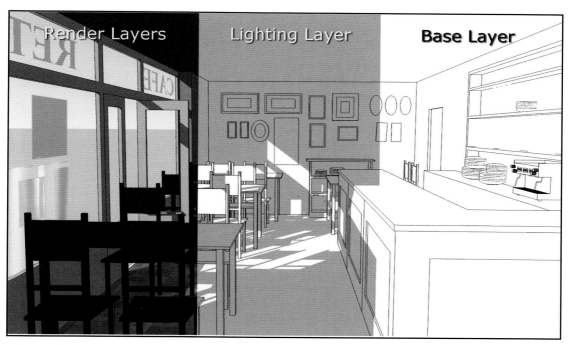

Here I have exported 3 different styles from Sketch-up (of the same model) and used them as separate layers in Photoshop. This can enable easy selection of all the elements for later rendering.

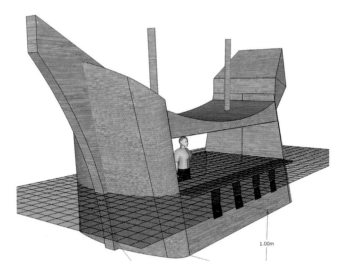

This pirate ship bar was just roughed out in 3D to aid the construction calculations (a template was required to create the full sized formers). A slice through grid was put in at 1m hieght. The grid squares could then be scaled up to full size.

1.00m

Left, the completed ship. Due to the restricted access, this had to be built in sections. Constructing the initial drawings in 3D, moved a lot of these complex curve dilemas to the drawing board as opposed to the contruction team, therefore saving on build time.

Rotating this same model into a desirable position, printing then tracing over a it embellishes the important details in the illustrations above. This is very quick and avoids drawing up the basic shape more than once when time is of the essence.

Final note on visuals: Try to avoid sending anything other than a simple 2D jpeg to the clients because; as with all drawings, the person at the other end may be a 'non techi' with a bad Internet connection and a black and white printer!' So the whole operation must be geared towards the end user. Construction drawings will be covered later in this book.

Mood Boards:

Mood boards are basically a selection of props, colours and materials presented in such a way as to suggest the overall look of the set. Here your stylist is crucial as props, when out of context, namely not on set, can be deceptive and often not seen for real by the designer until the dress day. An experienced stylist will probably whizz around the prop houses in record time accumulating hundreds of photos of 'might do's' in the eternal hunt for a specially requested item. It's often the easiest item that proves the most difficult to find because it's either 'out of season' or 'sold out, expecting more soon'. I do not envy their job. It's also very handy to have a scale reference taken on unusually small or large props. This can be achieved by including a tape measure or ruler positioned next to the prop being photographed.

I once ordered what I thought was a small conch shell from photos supplied for dressing a window alcove only to find it requiring 4 people to lift off the truck as it was huge!

Broadly speaking, art directors would like as many choices as possible of all props, yet too many can lead to confusion. Sometimes just one prop can set the whole thing off. Having said this, some of my most challenging jobs have been where the client has insisted it's simple and should be cheap because it only requires one prop!

After a few days research we should be in possession of many possibilities. It is important to file these correctly as most communication is on the phone and your file names should be consistent. I tend to create a file for each prop house, import the photos, and then create a file within this named 'I Like'. The good ones are then 'copied' as opposed to 'moved' into this file. This way makes it easier to locate the original prop and where it came from.

It would be relatively easy just to e-mail the photos direct to the client. But presenting it in an orderly way makes it much simpler and more professional for all concerned. Mood boards are an excellent communication tool especially in meetings. An evening spent creating A4 sheets for each set and pasting the props up creatively in Photoshop soon follows. Place numbers on all the photos so the client can remotely discuss individual props and attach any other samples or colour swatches accordingly.

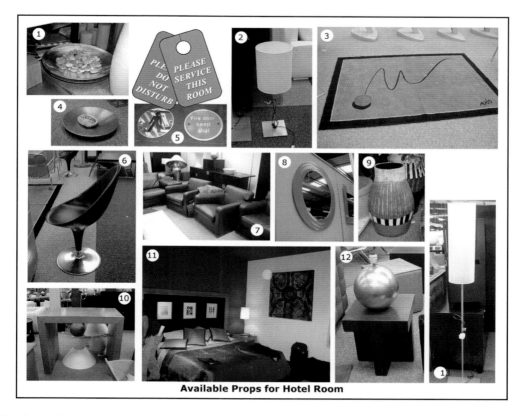

Available Props for Hotel Room

This board is created to show the available choices of props for a hotel room set. Try to number all the photos to ease communication during the job.

Drawing to scale:

Construction drawings are created as a communication tool for the construction team and should include scale elevations and plans plus of course a stage layout.

Traditionally this is the job for the draughtsperson using a drawing board to create eventual dyeline prints. Now created on computer the task is made much simpler and is often done by the set designer, especially on smaller jobs.

I've always tended to do my own drawings but now must admit to being converted to 3D Sketch-up Layout (supplied with the pro version).

Early CAD programs were designed for architects, as opposed to designers, and the detail was often far too great and time consuming. Conversely, cheap 'design your own home' 3D programs don't allow enough flexibility for our individual needs. If we need a door, we don't want to specify the thickness or fire spec, nor do we have 6 months to learn the program, we just want a door!

Construction drawings don't need to be that complicated for many filming jobs, unless of course on larger productions. The designer, or assistant is usually on hand at the build to help with queries, and the structure generally has less need for longevity. Film carpenters should be experienced enough to interpret what's required without the need for extra details to confuse. The important stuff is; How high, what length, which window and how far away from the cyc? In simple terms that means; 1 x side view, 1 x front view and 1 x plan view, preferably to scale, with another drawing showing the set position on the stage floor.

Sketchup-Layout has the advantage of being able to create a pdf file and print it to scale, unlike many basic cad programmes which; when printed, automatically adjust the size of image to fit the printer's margins. This is useful as it's impossible to put every dimension on a plan and a carpenter can measure off your drawing in your absence. It is also worthwhile including a perspective view within the construction drawing for ease of understanding.

The other obvious advantage with Sketch-up is being able to create your visual, your construction drawings and of course, see your set in 3D before spending lots of money. All in one program, so you save time. You can edit one element and it affects all the rest accordingly.

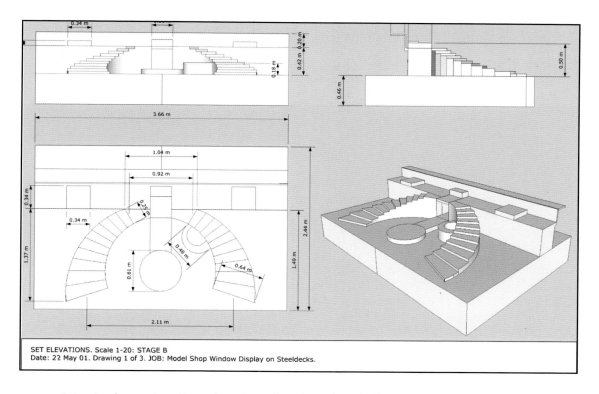

A typical construction drawing showing details for a model rostrum set. Perspective detail, though not imperative, can be very useful for quick assessment of the job.

What size should the set be:

Scenery for movies, TV dramas and multi camera productions require pretty much a complete and realistic set, yet after the edit we might only see one corner. This can be extremely frustrating spending time and money on things not featured or even seen. It occurs far too often but I guess it's the final straw of flexibility provided for the director in order to remain creative. Good 3D CAD software can be adjusted to lens specification and this information needs to be gathered at the earlier briefs and subsequent meetings. A director or DOP may prefer filming with wide lenses, which will mean both ceilings and floor come more into shot. Conversely, on wide lenses, much of the background can appear diminished, reducing the need for excessive detail. If filming on long lenses the detail may occasionally come into sharp focus accentuating any possible faults, yet ceilings may not be required. Much of this can be calculated in advance given certain information, even without a computer which can be especially useful if one is working in a small or restricted space. Scenery is inherently expensive and with all departments facing scrutiny one needs to be efficient. Knowledge of the aspect ratio of the final film is essential but it's wise to gather further information like the ideal lens choice. *I once had to quote on a set, shot from high up on a large crane with a maximum height of 25m, using a 35mm lens. The crane was only to be booked for one day, so calculations were imperative in advance of booking it, to establish how big the set should be, and therefore how much it might cost.*

On the following page is a nomogram, which gives an approximate width each lens will see at a set distance. Providing you have lens specification, shot width, or distance (any two of the three), you can determine the other ideal. In other words, what will be seen through the lens. This, I have found tremendously helpful in the past and has saved on both build time and budget. It also works for projecting on to screens etc. and is especially handy for large-scale projections.

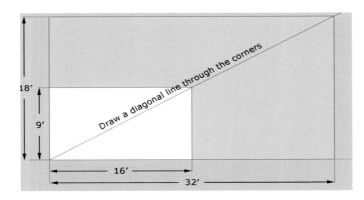

If you are aware of the format (ie. with a 9 x 16 aspect ratio), a 32' wide view will be 18' high, (see left). This can be used to show how much foreground floor will be in shot, by drawing an elevation once screen height is established. See following images.

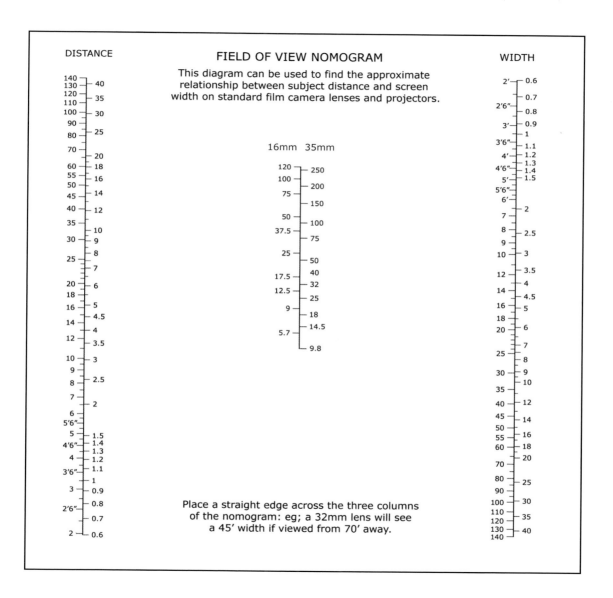

DISTANCE

FIELD OF VIEW NOMOGRAM

This diagram can be used to find the approximate relationship between subject distance and screen width on standard film camera lenses and projectors.

WIDTH

16mm 35mm

Place a straight edge across the three columns of the nomogram: eg; a 32mm lens will see a 45' width if viewed from 70' away.

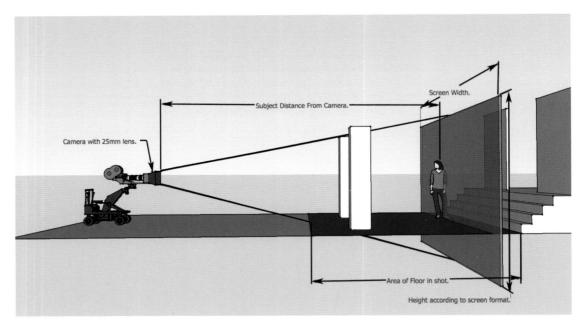

The image above shows a typical scenario where one needs to calculate an area of flooring. By measuring the distance of the actress (subject) from the camera, the width can be calculated from the previous nomogram. This then dictates the height, according to film format (area in blue). Once this is placed on the set elevation, your floor will run out where the line strikes it. This method can be used in numerous ways and is especially useful when calculating ceiling sizes prior to building.

PROPS

An introduction to Props:

A stylist or prop buyer would normally research and source the props and prop houses are by far the most ideal place to start. These are mainly centered around large film centres like London, Manchester and Hollywood. There are too many to mention here but annual publications similar to 'Kay's Art Department', 'The Knowledge' in Europe and LA 411 in America have listings of all the main prop houses. These prop houses mostly specialise in their own particular theme such as 'musical instruments' or 'period furniture'. They have websites displaying a broad range of their items, though these are rarely comprehensive. If a supplier is not able to help with a specific prop they are usually aware of other companies who might help so no harm is done in asking and tapping their comprehensive knowledge.

If a suitable item is found, photograph it and check it is available for your shoot dates. The Supplier will then issue a job number and check your clients' payment

Some larger prop houses carry a huge choice of alternatives that can overwhelm the uninitiated.

record (they usually hold blacklists of bad payers). All being well it will be penciled for your production, and booked following payment or a company order form.

Shops are another useful source for props but care should be taken to negotiate carefully the rental or purchase price. If the shop is prepared to hire, 20% of the item's replacement value is generally a good starting point for negotiations. If an item is unique the fee may be more and should it be damaged, whether in transit or on the shoot, you could be charged it's full replacement value. It is also known for shops to sell items prior to rental so 'make sure you've got it'. There have been occasions where E bay has been useful, but individual transport and storage for many items can be time consuming and prohibitive. Internet purchasing can be by far the cheapest but be wary of their delivery times as despite their promises, by the time it gets to the dispatch department, anything can happen. It may seem expensive but you would be far better paying extra for secure next day delivery to be sure of a reliable service. I have had many an agonizing time waiting for late arrivals in the post the day before the shoot!

Small items are known as 'smalls' and can be difficult to estimate on a big set. It's often useful to just calculate the overall runs or lengths of dressed shelves, especially with books, which are hired by the 'foot/metre', or 'bumph' (loose paperwork and files) as hired in boxes. Checking off then becomes simpler when each item is not individually listed.

Any practical electrical item will need PAT testing to be sure it's safe to use. This is a standard test carried out by a specially qualified electrician. A sticker is applied showing when it was last tested and how long before re-test (usually every job). Sometimes the prop houses will PAT test at a small extra charge, or even for free. If not, a quick call to the gaffer prior to your shoot can secure a qualified electrician to test props on the rig day.

All electrical devices on set will need PAT testing prior to use.

The only way to avoid PAT testing is to purchase items brand new, which is obviously not possible for period items. If a lot of lights are involved, get it done on your shoot, with fewer items, ask the prop house to do it for you prior to delivery if possible.

Prop Disposal:

You can almost guarantee that any useful purchased props will have found a home by the end of the day but many of the large or awkward items can present a problem. Occasionally prop houses might express an interest but this may incur extra transport costs or storage. As designers we often have this dilemma and before long we wish we had never volunteered to assist by just taking it home to store at our premises, which get more and more cluttered with items we never really want! This is one good reason for us, as designers, never to have anything larger than a small car, to avoid getting lumbered. We would be better saying that the prop has served its purpose and should be binned, sad though that may be. A special note here, if an item needs to be kept for possible future filming or continuity, that is the production's dilemma, not the designer's. Whatever I've been asked to look after has rarely been used again and on the occasion it has, there have been transport or insurance dilemmas costing me time, money and stress!

Prop Handling:

An experienced prop driver can be a huge advantage on set. Firstly they know where all the prop houses are and how they work. They can also load the props in shoot order so a 'full' truck doesn't necessarily need unloading all on your first location where say just one or two props are required! They can assist with checking off and even helping to dress if required. I was once coming to the end of a job filming in numerous locations when during a quiet spell, the driver suggested we check off all the props from the last two weeks filming. This was to save doing it in the dark upon wrap. We unloaded all the props on the grass and spent the next two hours checking off, wrapping, packing then loading back on the truck in order for a smooth return. Many other crew were also sitting on the grass just chatting including the producer who approached us and said, "Excuse me, I've been watching for a while and don't understand what you are all doing" He was totally unaware that this process happened on every job, but usually on a strike day in his absence, and was amazed at the amount of work involved. It is a job that is necessary to avoid loss and damage charges to the production!

Propman:

A specialist prop man usually organizes the prop handling. From the moment props arrive he will assume responsibility for their care and safety. If on a stage the prop man usually handles the stage keys and will open up and be last out in order to keep the props safe. He will also carry a kit (amongst others) for cleaning, polishing and general care of the props.

A good prop man can be an indispensable asset on any production. Here Chris Brett displays his well-used kit. Ask for anything, prop related, and you can be sure he has it, plus tools to make it if required.

When contracting a propman, you buy not only their vast experience in packing, arranging, lifting and dressing of props, but access to all their cleaning kit, crew chairs, weather cover, dust sheets, aerosols and virtually every item you may have forgotten. They will also take care of prop continuity and put valuable props away from prying eyes once shot.

If budget won't allow for a prop man and there are very few props, it is taken care of by the designer or his assistant. Prop houses have special areas where items are checked, packed and unpacked. From here van drivers pick up the paperwork, pick up the props, and return them.

When the props arrive on set, a safe area should be allocated where they can be unwrapped and checked off. A few props tables are helpful so all can be done at working height. Keep all the boxes and wrapping under your tables for the future returns. It may seem a fruitless task checking off items that have just been unloaded but if an item is missing or damaged, yet on the delivery note, you can be sure to be charged for it even though it never arrived. Open up all the props and then check off each item with their appropriate note. Also, note any damage.

Create a clear working area prior to unpacking and check carefully for any damage prior to use, otherwise you may be charged in error.

A simple phone call to the prop house notifying of any loss or damage can save any future discrepancies. Usually, there is a combination of purchases and rented props so it is a good idea to mark these items for future reference (after a few days filming it's easy to get confused on their return). Another idea may be to photograph the recently unpacked props for ease of re-packing at the wrap.

All legitimate production companies should have your props insured from the moment they are picked up to when they are returned. However; it's wise to check cover with them should you pick up the items personally by car, as there have been cases of insurers refusing to pay out when personal transport has been used.

SET DRESSING

On Set Dressing:

 On larger productions specialist set dressers are employed to dress the scene working closely with the prop man but on smaller jobs it's down to the designer and possibly an assistant.

For the first time all the preparation done over the past few days or weeks can be seen in context, and like many other tasks this needs to be done methodically.

Prepping For Exterior Locations:

Exterior locations can potentially be a designer's nightmare, mainly because one can't control the elements. However when the script or budget dictates, we need to be as prepared as possible. One of the greatest problems in most countries is the weather and with insurance adding up to a third of the total budget, it is rare to get extra shoot days. I would recommend the following checklist for a designer or construction manager:

Weather: Check the day before (as that's when it's most accurate) so you can prepare as much as possible. This must also include hats and sun cream for the summer and coats for the winter for you. Extra tarpaulins or even rope (for wind) are worth considering. Winter locations suffer from very short daylight hours so torches are essential. Plus, if you can get power, work-mans lights. Frost is a common problem especially with hired plants and these can be ruined if left uncovered overnight, or even on a van, so protect them.

Catering: As with all locations on a low budget there are rarely any facilities laid on for the prep crew, or art dept. If you haven't prepared for this, the crew finding say 'the nearest café' or other facility will take extra time. It's often wise to arrange some basic catering to keep your crew on site for longer. A willing and resourceful location manager might offer to help but they are not obliged to. Keep the receipts for claiming any expenses incurred.

Security: I've prepped on many sites only to find tools or props miraculously disappear. *On one South African job we even had the toilet rolls disappear during the 12-day build, only to find it was our security guard who was stealing them!* But be especially careful with props; punters just love to take souvenirs, and it will inevitably be the most vital and difficult to replace item that goes missing.

Bin: Sounds obvious but crew, especially clients, have generally just popped to Costa Coffee or similar prior to arriving on set and highlighting rubbish bins can at least cut down on some of the clearing up. I find the garden centre 'pop up bins' especially useful for this, but make sure you get the 'large' liners to fill them.

Contact Sheet: The shoot call sheet may not be finished or include all of the build and prep crew so it's wise to have every one's numbers should people get lost.

Movement order: This should be the location manager's task and should include numbers for local police and hospital as well as a FULL postal code for Sat-navs. If given the chance I will note any local hardware store locations passed, for the inevitable return later during the build to pickup spare materials or tools.

Long Electrical Extension Lead: Always useful even if just to charge the cordless tools. It's good practice to try to be as self sufficient as possible.

First Aid Kit: This should be carried by at least one member on site.

Fire Extinguisher: I always carry a small one in my car but larger may be necessary to be left on site (these can be hired).

Dressing Exterior Locations:

It's all very job dependent but here are a few tips I've learnt over the years. It might sound obvious, but do check you have permission to do whatever is required. I was once supposed to be having scaffolding erected on a town hall only to find out that permission from the freeholder, as opposed to the tenants, had not been sought.

On another embarrassing occasion, packing up after a shoot, we inadvertently found out that the location owner's wife had not informed her own husband about the filming we had just completed, hoping to pocket the cash. Because the shoot ran late, the husband returned home from work, and was, understandably quite furious!

One tip is to make sure whatever you are fixing can be easily and quickly removed, cable ties are ideal as they can be cut away. Its also worthwhile having some camouflage netting available, to cover any unsightly objects. This can be quite cheap to hire or buy.

Tree branches often used to break up the light are called 'Dingle'. Try to cut these sensibly so as not to damage the source tree, also, if trying to be discreet, cover your fresh cut branches with dirty water or mud to disguise your actions.

Always have at hand some polythene sheeting for weather changes. Even if your kit is under cover there will be some other department requiring protection. Ezy-up tents are ideal but again expensive. Stating the obvious but there may be no power supply so try to keep to manual or battery tools.

The wrap usually occurs when the light fails, therefore leaving your strike team in the dark, prepare for this by gathering all tools and props in one place and have your torches to hand.

Street Dressing:

We are often asked to dress areas of the highway and put up signage etc.. This task can be made less stressful by hiring freestanding signposts on their own metal bases. Anything from bus stands to working traffic lights are available. Some small wedges are useful to level these up, as most pavements are uneven. White lines, traffic lights and zebra crossings are available in specialist prop houses, road markings are in pre cut painted rubber. It may seem a cheap option to paint these but tarmac can be wet; especially first thing in the morning, and paint may be difficult to remove after the shoot.

Vehicles:

It is sometimes wise to hire some prop car number plates for sticking onto action vehicles. Get these from the vehicle suppliers, as it's now illegal (in the UK) to have them made up without the necessary vehicle documents. Remember, you shouldn't film other people's cars without their consent.

Ageing Down: Most vehicles, especially if rented from private owners, have been cleaned and polished immaculately just prior to filming. This is rarely required so we need to know how realistically to age them down. The best way to achieve this is to drive them through some muddy puddles or to mix up some real dirt in water, to make mud, and splatter with a large paintbrush. Actually paint it, as opposed to splatter, should you require a more subtle ageing but take care as it does dry a different colour. Specialist water based 'dirty down' aerosols are available but expensive. Also try dirty water in a small spritzer, though the dirt can block the spritzer nozzle.

I've often found a roll of sign writer's vinyl useful for covering van logos; this comes in many colours, and in low tack. Magnetic vinyl is another option which can even be pre printed, these are often used on company vans, but remember, it doesn't stick to plastic.

Note: If sticking logos or vinyl onto vehicles. Rub in some petroleum jelly onto the surface area first. This will hold it on yet not stick fast for ease of removal afterwards.

Interior Locations:

Interior locations are a popular choice for those on limited budgets. There are obvious benefits but they can bring their own set of problems. Primarily the location owner has put his premises on the 'locations list' for just one of two reasons.

To generate extra income to cover his bills, or because he is so overly proud of the location and he wants to display it to the world.

In my opinion the financial saving in not needing to build a set is often compromised by the cost of the extra time required physically to film the location. This is rarely adequately accounted for in shoot schedules. Equipment and crew can soon swamp a normal sized room and every shot requires moving kit or cables before it can be dressed, lit and rehearsed. A decent DOP will often struggle to obtain even mediocre lighting because of light-stands being in shot etc.

It's inevitable that some sort of damage will occur and as a result the art department should provide some preventative measures.

Most damage is accidental however, if the art dept are not made aware, say from the light stand hitting the ceiling, they get called back afterwards. Far more preferable to deal with the situation upon the wrap or during a quiet time on the shoot so, for other crewmembers, please let us know straight away!

Floor protection:

We used to fit 'Essex board', a compressed 1/8"cardboard in 8' x 4' sheets, called such because it was easy to lay. This has been superseded by 'Cordek' (a corrugated plastic sheet the same size, supplied in black or white) because these sheets are even easier to cut and cheaper to buy. If I were to choose quality over price the former is far more absorbent making it ideal for those occasional wet days, it's also better for sound. There is always a constant flow of crew from out to in and something absorbent prevents wet mud coming in. Shoe protectors are a complete waste of time because there is always someone who feels too important to use them or simply forgets when leaving the room. Cordek is very useful for blacking out windows though as unlike drapes, it's okay in the rain and fixes up painlessly as it's self-supporting.

In order to do any of the above it is advisable to get into the location at least an hour before the crew arrive so all can be cleared and the floor laid. At this stage it's worth remembering that those fitting the floor are entering overtime one hour earlier than the main crew (for budgetary reasons).

Dressing Interior Locations:

Try to start with a blank canvas by keeping your props in a separate area prior to dressing in. Dress carpets and flooring first followed by the larger items, window dressing, and then the wall pictures and lights. A prop man or assistant is useful here as it's wise to observe from afar before drilling holes in the walls. All this followed by the shelf decoration and smalls. At this stage it can be incredibly frustrating having clients all putting in their oar. I would much prefer they let me finish, and then have their say, however, it's their project too.

Note: If creating a busy wall of pictures, it is wise to layout all the pictures, in their correct positions on the floor prior to fixing so their layout appears more structured.

Many of the pictures and curtains will require wire and fixings, which should be with your prop man, if not they should be in your toolkit. If fixing to flattage, heavy items should have a wooden 'pad' on the reverse. However on real walls it can be more difficult as it depends on using existing fixings or being given permission to drill holes into their property. There are some so called 'invisible' fixings available in hardware stores but these will still possibly damage paintwork or worse plasterwork, always check with the owner at recce stage. An often-simpler option is to offer to fill and repaint a whole wall or room once you have done your drilling and fixing.

When fitting nets or curtains on location it's wise to measure the length required at the recce, then buy a telescopic rod from a curtain supplier, this should fit in the reveal safely without damage as they are wedged in. These are available in different lengths. Failing this, a length of dowel fixed with a small rubber 'doorstop' wedge may suffice using the existing wall curtain fixtures to hide your efforts.

It's wise to secure a safe area for the storage of the owners' furniture and crew equipment. This should be proposed at the recce. Take extra care when moving items to other rooms, this is where damage is often done. Space is usually an issue on shoots so it may be worth considering storing it in a warehouse whilst filming or even under polythene outside.

Note: When moving heavy items on a hard floor. Always slide as opposed to lift by placing the item on a dustsheet or blanket. When in position, remove the blanket; this should prevent scratching the floor.

Take photos on your first day before any work takes place, especially if you see any existing damage. If accused later of something for which you are not responsible, you then have the evidence.

A crack in the ceiling and a glass panel is photographed prior to shoot to avoid possible unnecessary repair.

Also always ask the director or DOP before cleaning any windows, as it's difficult to replicate good dirt when required. The windows may need a 'neutral density' or 'ND' gel applying to reduce the light intensity from outside. This should be done and supplied by the electrical dept but the art dept is often asked to assist to avoid bubbles and wrinkles. This is either applied with tape and or staples which can easily cause damage to the window frames so care must be taken to choose the correct tape, or the right length staples (very short are recommended here, to pull out easily with the gel upon removal).

Differentiating between the owners props above and your hired ones can be confusing after a shoot so try to mark all with coloured self adhesive stickers.

Shoot days are often long and it's easy to forget what came from where at the days end. If the majority of the props you are dressing with belong to the owner, mark those you've brought in or visa versa. Little coloured stickers from your local stationary store are ideal for this task. The initial photos are also useful for re dressing the house when you are wrapping so print them out before your last shoot day for the wrap team.

STUDIOS

 There will be a time when one has had enough of location filming and compromising with lens choice in order to squeeze into a space, and this is where the studio comes in. Studios, though appearing expensive initially, can save considerable shoot time as one is working in controlled conditions. Ceilings or walls can be removed in the set to allow for better lighting and camera positions, sound is no longer interrupted etc.   There are various types of studios available, some purpose built, some just large spaces suitable for filming. In city centres, where space a premium, the cost will be high and the space is often restricted, especially for car parking and truck deliveries so choice of locations becomes paramount. Virtually every professional film will need parking for trucks and cars. Other restrictions could be that one needs sound deadening or increased power for special lighting or that it even needs to be close to an airport for the talent or client.

Listed on the following pages are the various types of studios in most countries.

Television Studios:

These are purpose built areas designed primarily for video and TV production. Sometimes they have collapsible audience seating and usually come with semi permanent lights fixed to the studio rig and a director's gallery (a separate room for multiple camera viewing/editing). They are air-conditioned and fully soundproofed and also have a smooth 'TV' floor suitable for tracking cameras. This may be a special 'rubberised' paint which you would be well advised NOT to cut on or damage. They also have tab tracks with pull around drapes of blue or black.

These facilities cost considerably more to run and therefore more to hire so scenery is usually prefabricated in workshops prior to building on stage to keep the costs down as stage rental cost can be prohibitive.

Film Studios:

These are again soundproofed and have a purpose built rig for hanging your own lights and scenery. Often they have wooden floors suitable for fixing onto, though these may not necessarily be level. Many of the smaller independent ones also have a cyclorama, or infinity cove (some solid and some just stretched canvas). The larger stages generally have no cyclorama (as maintenance becomes an issue) and time will be required if one is needed to hang and prime (add, on average, two days onto build time). As the film lights are brought in specifically for the shoot, stage hire charges can be less than TV studios and set building can start directly on the stage as a result.

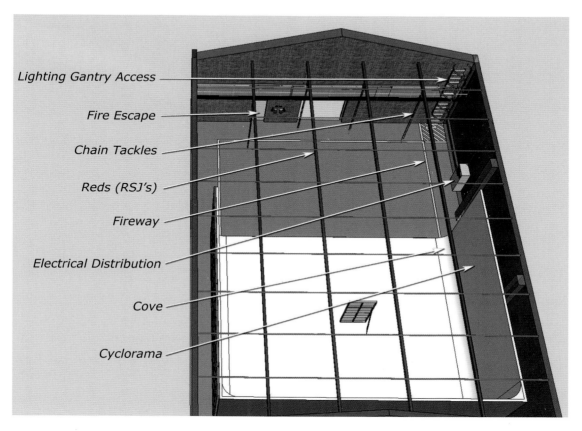

Lighting Gantry Access

Fire Escape

Chain Tackles

Reds (RSJ's)

Fireway

Electrical Distribution

Cove

Cyclorama

A typical small Film Studio layout. Always keep the fireways clear.

Specialist Car Studios:

These are designed specifically for cars with total wrap around cycloramas and overhead ceilings to reduce in car reflections. The good stages have these on electric hoists for ease of operation and moveable wheel jacks to ease the car movement.

Stills Studios:

Often considerably smaller, these are generally 'large rooms' with natural overhead light and blackout blinds. As lights and camera equipment are usually stored on site, dustsheets are useful and great care should be taken when building and painting to protect the floor and equipment.

Converted Studios:

These are warehouses or large buildings converted to create a filming space within. They sometimes have their own cyclorama, cove and wooden floor with a basic scaffolding rig fixed to the existing roof structure. Lack of good soundproofing can be a problem though (often eased by hanging blackouts) but these studios are generally a bit cheaper allowing for this. They can often be a bit lower in height and can have fewer facilities than purpose built studios.

Some basic studio terms:

Four Waller:

This is a basic stage with no other facilities such as light or camera rental, in house catering or construction crew. You have to get everything in yourself.

Running a studio can be expensive and studio managers often offer some extra services to help keep them more profitable like lighting or camera kit. It also means they can offer 'studio deals' provided you use 'their' equipment.

Cyc or "Cyclorama":

This is the wrap around wall (often referred to as an infinity cove) to give an apparently seamless look enabling the floor to 'disappear' into the walls.

These can be solid wood, with plywood or plaster/glassfibre curves in the corners, or scenic canvas hung between scaffolding and stretched around the corners. The latter is generally cheaper but requires more frequent replacement (too many coats of paint degrades the cloth eventually).

Drapes:

These are made up as large curtains and usually run on tab tracks (a heavy duty curtain rail) around the stage edge. They are normally black but occasionally white or chroma key blue. It is obviously not possible for a cove around the floor.

Rig:

This is a special structure installed in the roof designed for hanging the lights and/ or scenery, usually fixed to the existing RSJ's in the building's structure.

Chain Tackles:

These are special hoists to enable lifting of scenery or lights. They generally run on RSJ's so can be moved whilst under load. They can be manually operated with a chain or electrically on a remote system.

Fire Way:

This is a marked clearway around the stage perimeter for fire protection which aids escape in the event of fire so should be left clear of obstructions at all times.

Reflector:

Often used in specialist car studios these are large overhead ceilings, sometimes electrically operated, to hang over the stage, particularly useful for reducing unwanted reflections in cars etc.

Stage Door:

This is the large access door required for loading and unloading scenery.

Tank:

A purpose built facility for using with water scenes, often sunken in the floor and with removable cover. When the tank is used handrails should be constructed around the perimeter to prevent accidents.

Strike:

A period of time dedicated to taking the set/lights down and generally clearing up.

Studio Etiquette:

Studios run a 'Pencil' system similar to booking film crew, so consider exactly how many days you require, including build and strike. They usually work on a 'ten hour' rental day with an hourly rate for any overtime (it might be just a brick box but someone has to stay there to lock up and look after the place). Bear in mind also that if you work late your transport often has to be done the following day and another company may have booked the space. So a strike day may be required.

1st Pencil: Your shoot dates are not yet committed to money but no other companies have expressed interest, and you may confirm the studio at any time.

2nd Pencil: You are written in the booking diary but another company has already pencilled similar dates, should they pull out, you are moved up to first pencil.

3rd Pencil: As above, but two other companies had pencilled before you.

Confirmation: You have confirmed these dates and are liable to a fee should you not turn up. This fee usually depends on the likelihood of the stage being re-booked to another company in the time available.

If you have a 1st pencil but the 2nd pencil company are willing to confirm, you are then obliged to confirm or you may loose creditability with that studio for future bookings and they will not offer you a 1st pencil again.

Despite your production seeming to be the most important thing on the planet, it is worth remembering that your booking, to the studio manager, is just another booking. So, should you want to go in early, work late, have something delivered out of hours or anything else, it is only courteous to let them know as often they run on a skeleton staff when not fully booked. Try too, to let them have at least a call sheet, and script so they know with whom to deal with.

Upon Arrival:

When you first arrive at the studio it should be clean and tidy with a clear floor space. Take note of this because YOU should leave it in the same state as when you arrived. Should you require the cyclorama painting by the studio this should have been completed, probably on the previous night.

Any catering will have been pre booked but teas and coffees should be available locally.

The art department are often the first in and should note how tidy the area is. There should be fire extinguishers and efficient lighting for work plus access to heat etc.

If anything unusual like explosives, fire, water effects, or vehicles are expected let them know, as special insurances might be required. Also a wet floor can be a disaster for a studio often requiring repair or complete replacement and lost bookings. You will be liable for any damage like this, if done on your production. You will also be liable for a cleaning charge should the space be left untidy or someone has blocked the sink.

Personal Experience:

Having spent a substantial part of my life helping to run, and working in, studios, I feel somewhat well qualified to write on this issue.

Running a film studio where one sees numerous construction companies, production companies, talent and crew may give the impression of being a rather glamorous career. Much of the time is spent juggling bookings, staff and deals amongst all the clients together with the day-to-day chores of regular maintenance and paying the bills. Companies and crew often complain that something is not right or something else isn't there. There are endless late nights care-taking and numerous hours spent painting the cyc or sweeping the floor. Glamorous it most certainly is not!

There was one interesting vantage point amongst the many tedious chores though. Many of the companies had their own unique way of working with each thinking they knew better than the others. A production company could be compared to a family with everyone knowing how the other works within their own group. This can work extremely effectively as with most companies but detrimentally with others.

A good freelancer (working for all) can possibly succeed in his career by being able to adjust their way of working to fit in with each company's various working practices, whether good or bad. It is also possible, after time, to judge fairly early on whether your day ahead will be a pleasure or a struggle!

When one rents an unknown studio, there are many important issues to consider. Various departments will each be thinking of their own needs so a recce is always advisable. I can speak here with experience having recently cut up a new set, to fit in the lift, after being told it was their largest studio in a well establised company!

Should you need the cyc colour changing ask the studio manager for a quote, this will often be cheaper than your own art department doing it as there will often be a stage rental deal as well and it could be done at night.

Producers should check exactly what they get for their money; usually things like heating and waste disposal are extra etc. How much will the power cost? If talent is expected check out the make up rooms and catering facilities plus Internet access, parking, distance to nearest airport etc.

It's often common practice for studios to reduce the daily rental charge but to load other services to give you the impression of a good deal.

Lighting; A decent DOP (and gaffer) should always be consulted prior to rental, he or she will be thinking of many issues like there being enough height and studio length for long shots, or whether the rig is suitable for hanging equipment and even if there is enough power.

Set; Any kind of set requires not just room but space behind windows and doors plus a reasonable floor to fix to. It needs to be warm and light for painting and paper drying. If water is being used proper filling and draining facilities will be required. Hanging rigs may be needed, plus access for large vehicles. Note: stages are usually only insured for action vehicles with 'nearly empty' fuel tanks.

Any professional dancers generally need purpose built sprung wooden floors and cannot perform properly, or safely, on a standard concrete floor.

Summarizing there are many different requirements for each individual shoot and stage choice should be a very significant decision not just dictated by the budget.

SCENERY

Set Construction, techniques and materials:

Throughout the years, from theatre to film, various techniques were used to achieve realistic looking sets that were lightweight, easy to handle and store. These techniques have been perfected over the years, especially with the introduction of newer, lighter materials that are designed specifically for scenery as opposed to 'general building'.

The most notable change in recent years has been the reduction in manpower as this has often been considered the most expensive element in the ever-increasing need to reduce budgets.

We as designers are often asked to achieve scenes from period replications right through to futuristic settings often dealing with unique and unusual materials.

It is for this reason that we choose well-used elements that can be utilized in unimaginable ways to create these scenes. Often hired and rebuilt in different ways, these elements are categorized below and are commonly used in our industry.

Flats:

Film sets are built to look authentic, they need to be lightweight, they need to be built quickly and they need to be cheap. Other considerations are being safe and easy to store etc. Wood is the most versatile of all materials, and as a result, the vast majority of sets are built from it. From the early days of theatre a technique was used to build 'flats' for the creation of scenery. All built around the same template, they can be joined together in numerous ways to create a lightweight wall of any size. The default size is 8' x 4' nowadays, however 9' x 4' and 10' x 4' are also commonly used.

A standard 8' x 4' flat consisting of thin plywood stiffened with timber and supported with a brace.

A flat is a thin sheet of plywood with stiffening battens fixed to the reverse enabling it to be light, strong and easily fixed together with others. In the past, for theatrical use, these were often held together with pin hinges as the joins were less important and quick/safe changeovers were necessary. On a film set they are initially laid face down on the floor, nailed together, then raised off the floor for finishing. In both cases, they can be stored and transported easily and used again and again, making them ecologically very efficient. However, there was one problem. Whenever painted or papered, it affected the smooth front surface making them age very quickly. This was initially resolved by covering in hessian and lining it with wallpaper prior to painting or applying a surface. As the hessian wasn't fixed to the face, the surface remained unaffected and the flats could be re used. The hessian, if damaged was replaced. The whole system was very effective but had one vital flaw, it was labour intensive and required the flattage to be stripped off from the last job prior to starting the build utilising valuable time waiting for the new paper to dry prior to the paint finish being applied.

As the price of manpower increased and materials improved the system has been modified.

Firstly, it is now possible to get quality scenic canvas in wider widths (as opposed to just 6' wide) and the manufacturing price of this is becoming cheaper. Fillers are built to 'fill' areas not covered by the flattage, like above and below windows and door linings. These are all placed face down on the floor and strapped together, then covered in one whole canvas then painted. The canvas stretches concealing all the joins and giving a perfect surface all in one go. This is much quicker and can reduce build time by as much as a day on many sets. Once finished with, the canvas can be stripped off and thrown away leaving the virgin flats for future use.

Once the walls are constructed special techniques are used to keep them rigid. Long timber lengths made into an L shape are fixed to the back of the flattage. These prevent bowing when moving. The wall is held upright with a brace. These can be either nailed to the floor or held with stage weights (see studio floors). Nails used here are deliberately 'not homed in' leaving the nail head pronounced for ease of release later.

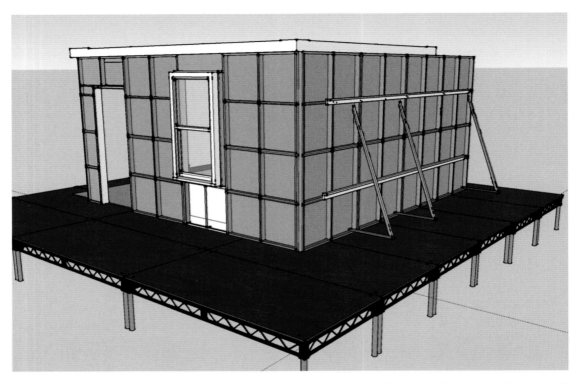

Set built on rostra seen from the back. A header and filler can be seen above and below the window.

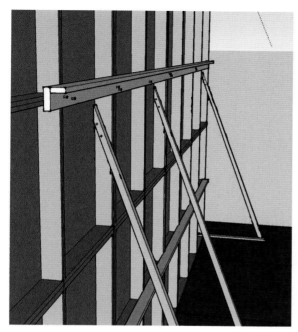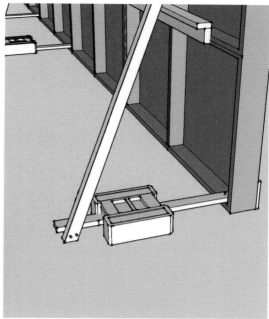

Details of straps and braces at the back of the flattage and the correct positioning of a stage weight. Note that the nails are not homed in for ease of strike out.

Ceiling Pieces:

Ceilings are usually built in one piece from a very large piece of canvas (usually 6 or 9oz) stretched over a wooden framework. This keeps them light and covers a large area. As they are so light and large they are often called 'Windbags' because they catch the wind whilst being carried between stages. It's often not necessary to cover the entire area of the set as it restricts the lighting possibilities and as it is relatively light it can be moved easily whilst on the set with the aid of brooms.

Note: When ordering the canvas always allow enough to pull around and tension material from the back i.e.: add approx 30cm all around.

Special techniques are used to build the frame to prevent any part of the canvas touching it when it is being painted, similar to those used on a small artists canvas. The drying canvas pulls bar tight and can often distort the frame if tensioned too much so biscuits are used in the corners and care should be taken when stretching and stapling to the back. All of these methods prevent permanent brush or roller marks on the canvas after drying.

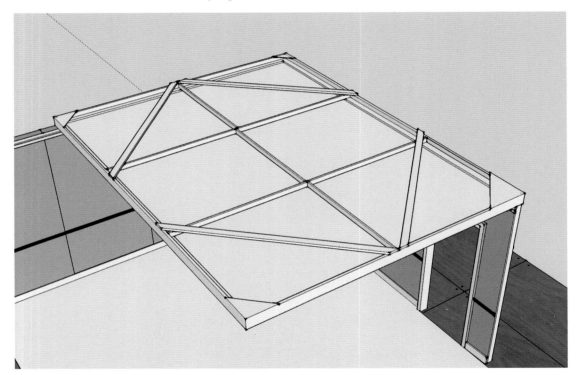

Detail of Ceiling Piece showing biscuits and straps.

If one needs to fit say a light or ceiling rose it's possible to fix a 3/4"plywood pad to the reverse by screwing it to one of the central battens behind. This is always best done with the ceiling piece down from the set so one can get to the back easily, and don't forget to drill a hole in the centre for the power supply.

Note: When hoisting ceiling pieces with hand lines always drill a fixing hole through the outside perimeter batten. If fixed to the inner timbers they may break loose, because here the nails are fixed into end grain of the timbers.

Flooring.

Flooring on a set is pretty much as you would expect, usually laid wood, carpet, or vinyl. As time is limited (you can't work on a set with a wet floor) any treatments are generally done at the day's end, and acrylic, as opposed to oil paints and glazes are preferred. It can be a big time saver to lay the floors prior to building the set as no 'cutting in' is required (a small set can always be prefabricated then lifted on) but protection is required during the rest of the build.

Traditional Temporary Stage Floor:

Hessian used to be laid straight onto the wood block base and stretched tight. This was then papered with heavyweight 4'wide 'kraft' paper which when dried was sealed and painted in any colour. This provided a seamless floor of any size and was also very good for dancers. It was easily ruined though with just one accidental cut or tear or any kind of large water spill. Nowadays tongue and grooved chipboard is used as it's quicker to lay but you still have the joins to overcome with paper or lino.

Dancers Floor:

Many experienced choreographers usually insist on a purpose built floor for any long routines. Dancers will soon tire on a concrete or TV floor (see Studios) and there is a risk of injury with anyone falling so a special 'sprung' floor should be laid. One solution is to lay strips of wood say every 1ft and lay a chipboard tongue & groove floor over this. This is enough to provide some bounce and protect their knees. Another possibility is to buy foam-backed vinyl as described below.

Note: On virtually every three walled set I've built I have had to order at least 20%-30% extra flooring as the camera often sees more floor when pulled out to see 100% of the walls. Also buy some extra for replacing damaged areas.

When joining vinyl or carpet; the heavy duty carpet tape can stick too much on the studio floor so always stick this ON TOP of wide masking tape for easy removal on the strike.

DO NOT CUT on a studio floor without a special 'hooked' blade or a protective board underneath to prevent damage.

Laminates:

As these are pre-finished and relatively cheap they are a good obvious choice for scenery flooring but they will usually need a 'sub floor' of tongue & groove chipboard as the basic studio floor is rarely smooth enough to lay on. They also generally take much longer than one might expect because set floors tend to be larger than normal rooms. They are not always good for tracking on either. Note: It's good practice to fix timber battens around a t & g floor to protect the tongues for potential future use.

Linoleum or Vinyl:

This again is pre-finished and very quick to lay (superb for television studios) and is available in a multitude of designs though it will need a sub floor in some stages. It is now possible to buy foam backed dance floors in plain colours, considerably reducing build time, however this is expensive.

Carpet:

Quite expensive but easy to lay, carpet is the sound man's favourite but can be a nightmare for the art dept as it marks so easily. Also any pattern needs matching up on the joins so order more than required to allow for this.

Self-adhesive stage vinyl:

This is a specialist wide sticky back plastic used extensively in TV shows. Fantastic for a pre-finished gloss surface but can be difficult to lay as it is temperature sensitive. It also needs a very smooth sub floor and special 'squeegees' to apply. It is available in 'high' or 'low' tack (I'm still not sure which is best) but if the studio gets very hot, when filming, and the very cold overnight, you can almost guarantee bubbles on your return! We once used space heaters during our build and laid this

83

on a large rostrum area and could do nothing to stop the bubbles, however, upon our return the following day it all stretched out perfectly due to the temperature becoming more constant.

Tiles:

Real tiles are best laid on to 2mm polystyrene sheet (available from paint shops in rolls as a backing to wallpaper) as this prevents them slipping yet takes out any floor undulations. Once laid they can be grouted as normal yet are easily removed on the strikeout. Always put boards on top prior to camera tracking as the tiles will crack under weight.

Printed Flooring:

Printed flooring has developed exponentially during the past few years making it a superb choice for set designers. Costs are reducing and choices are increasing for off the shelf designs. Companies like 'Rutters' can print bespoke designs. Products like 'Flotex', using high definition printing onto flock, have anything from tiling to antique pine boards available off the shelf. This is remarkably realistic yet superbly quiet for the aid of the sound dept and it can be re-used.

Painted Canvas:

Quite good as you can have any design, but this will take ages to dry if stretched and painted in situe as it requires priming prior to any finished coat. Far better to paint off site, roll up when dry and re-lay within the set at the last minute.

Loose Canvas or old gauze (see also drapes later in this chapter):

This can be fantastic for any 'messy' sets and outdoor scenes in a studio. Just draped loosely over any undulations it contains all the leaves and dirt making for an easy strikeout. It also is not too slippery, unlike plastic sheeting, so can 'hold' top dressing better. Try to pre-paint it (before laying) in the shadow colour, or another dark colour so as to reduce the amount of top dressing required. It can be quite difficult to locate though as it's often thrown away so take a look in the studio skip, or save one from the last job. I've used gauzes quite often for creating background sand dunes in desert sets as this stretches around the cut outs or undulations similar to the real thing. It is a very useful alternative, as real sand is very heavy, and doesn't make good dunes in a studio as it won't build up enough hieght.

Rostra:

Rostrums are a quick and easy way to provide a platform for either camera, set or actors. Traditionally made from wood, the bases (known as 'gate legs'), all different heights, used to fold out and a purpose built 6' x 4' top would fit neatly on top providing a platform. This was a very efficient system but the bases required maintenance and were expensive to make, plus they trapped your fingers when folded up.

Metal rostrums have now superseded the traditional gate leg with the most popular being made by Steeldeck. These are a standard 8' x 4' metal framework with a 3/4" plywood top. The height can be adjusted by using alternative pre-cut steel tubes bolted in plus they can be bolted to each other.

Note: Always bolt the legs in, as they tend to fall out when the rostrum is lifted or moved.

Steel decks are much stronger (and heavier) but can support heavier items. The tops can also be easily replaced when damaged. Now available in smaller sizes, even circular, they have become an industry standard. It's also possible to fit wheels making them a very versatile piece of kit.

As these are popular their tops are rarely smooth, and they might require cladding. This is usually done in mdf and fixed down with nails or pneumatic staples/pins.

Above. A steel-deck rostrum is the industry standard in the UK. The legs are available in different heights making them extremely versatile.

Note: When cladding rostrums, always ensure the nails or staples are a suitable length to pull out WITH the cladding as opposed to staying in the rostrum top. Charges are sometimes incurred to make the top safe for future use to other customers and protruding nails or staples can cause injury. Check that all the feet are level (with pads on the floor) and overlap the existing rostrum joins with the cladding so as to provide a smoother surface. Vertical cladding can be carefully screwed into the plywood edge but the base of vertical joins need a pad on the reverse to fix to.

Any rostrum area built has a risk of crew falling off so it is strongly advised to build a suitable handrail wherever possible or provide a safe area within say 5' of the edge. If this precaution is not followed the designer may be liable for any accidents that occur.

Rostrums above 3' in height may require extra scaffolding to hold them rigid.

Turntables:

These are generally hired and can be sourced in any standard diameter. They usually come complete with their own motor and rheostat. Care must be taken to put them on a level base. If constructing your own turntable take care to buy 'locked' wheels as opposed to 'swivel' as the latter can lock if counter rotation is required.

Basic Rigging:

Rigging is used to support large or especially heavy scenery pieces. It is a specialised trade and there are grades within the rigging department which reflect their experience. All riggers should have liability insurance and be able to work with scenery or lights. This trade is especially helpful when working outdoors with external elements, like wind and rain, also if working at heights. For small jobs, riggers will usually come with their own equipment (scaffolding, towers, lines etc.) and sometimes a mate, and complete the job for a set price. Health and safety is a primary concern here, and their advice should be taken seriously.

Once a set wall or ceiling becomes too large to lift, it is advisable to rig scaffolding on the back and support it from above. A rigger will fix scaffolding (usually alluminum as opposed to steel) to the reverse, it will then be pulled up with hand lines or chain tackles if it's really heavy. Large purpose built film studios have RSJ's running across the stage rig (often called 'Reds' as they are painted red). These chain tackles roll on the Rsj's, which makes them very useful for moving large items across the stage, mid shoot, avoiding breakage and saving valuable floor space. If there aren't enough chain tackles on one beam, they can be easily 'tripped' from another beam. Once in position the structure can be 'made safe' with more scaffolding, either from the floor or the studio rig.

Riggers tend to work with either the art or electrical department (depending on who employed them). If 'sharing' a rigger between departments you will find they tend to prioritize according to who contracted them. If it is the electrical dept, be sure to ask in plenty of time if their help is required so they can prioritize.

Flying Sets:

Specialist riggers are employed for this service where, once scaffolding is fixed to the back of the set, it's wired up to pulleys and then down to counterweights. The position of these counterweights, when on the floor, needs to be clearly marked and roped off to prevent crew walking underneath should the wires fail, or the set be released. As previously said (re Grades), the only people insured to work on this kind of work are 'Wire riggers'. Wire riggers also work with special effects and Kirby wires for suspending actors.

When pricing up for this type of work you will find that their insurance will only allow for newly supplied and tested wire and cable.

SET MATERIALS

 The range of materials used for scenery is vast and the following is by no means comprehensive. However, there are certain criteria that differentiate between what's good for scenery and what's not. Scenery is usually only required for short-term use, it needs to be light and especially quick to create. It also needs to be adaptable and fireproof. The following list represents the most commonly used materials in our industry and gives advice on working with them and sourcing.

Timber:

By far the most commonly used material, as it's so versatile. It comes in various lengths, sheets and composites (wood chippings glued together into sheets) and is available in any location.

The large DIY chains tend to be the cheapest but sometimes the lowest quality. The timber is generally available in PP (pre-planed) or 'sawn' (rougher, just cut surface) and it's often difficult to find one straight piece out of a bundle. It's also usually sourced from the cheapest lower quality trees with numerous knots reducing its strength. Professional builders merchants are a better option, as the wood is normally superior quality, therefore stronger and straighter. They will also frequently match or better the price of the large DIY stores, especially for bulk orders.

When ordering timber. Bear in mind that 2" x 1"(or 1" x 2"in USA) will not be that exact size. Basically it was that size prior to planing, or should be. This means that if you order PP grade it will generally be 1/4" less in both directions. This varies according to supplier with the DIY chains being smaller still.

Should you require 'finished size' it will cost extra and will need ordering.

Most large studio complexes also have their own timber suppliers which stock specialist 'film' mouldings, a much superior product, where one can even order 'scenic batten' a special size developed for use on flattage and stretching canvas etc.

TV studios and theatre builds require all the above to be painted in fireproof paint.

The most widely used sheet material in UK scenery has to be MDF (Medium density fibreboard), which provides a very smooth surface yet is very easy to cut. This also comes in various grades, even waterproof but for scenery we usually have the softest and cheapest. MDF should be avoided in flattage though, due to its excessive weight. Special bendy MDF is also useful, but expensive. This is smooth one side and has a 'ribbed' pattern on the other to allow for bending which is good for making columns etc.

Flattage is usually constructed from plywood as it's lightweight as well as strong. This comes in various grades, and thicknesses, making it ideal for bending around formers. Thicker 19mm or 3/4" boards are ideal for flooring or strength. Another relatively cheap flooring option is Tongue & Groove chipboard which is ideal if a secondary floor is needed on an uneven stage floor. It fits together on its tongues and provides a good base for pre finished 'click' together laminates. This can also be re-used, however weight again becomes an issue especially in the delivery truck and the tongues often get damaged with re-use.

CNC cutting:

This process (computer numerical control), though relatively new, is ideal for cutting pre-defined shapes like intricate designs from boards. Once a design is created in CAD it can be transferred directly into the machine, which cuts and shapes automatically therefore saving valuable labour time. This technique is fantastic for repeat designs, though still cost prohibitive outside the workshop.

Metal:

Metalwork is a specialist trade requiring special tooling. Being very adaptable it is often a good option for sets in television that may require constant re-building, transporting and storage. Specialist companies have facilities to form all shapes and sizes, but different equipment is required depending upon the metal used. It's relatively cheap to weld and bend normal steel, but aluminum and stainless steel are more difficult and worth checking with the metalworker prior to ordering. Once machined, the welds often require polishing to remove tarnishes and sealing if being seen by camera.

Fake metalwork:

This can be achieved by painting normal MDF in bright silver and burnishing with a black metal polish like 'Zee bright'. When recreating metal with timber by spraying, the grain is enhanced so MDF, is best for simulating the surface. This is often useful when matching timber with metal. Make sure the end grain is well sealed prior to treatment otherwise it will show in a different colour. Another useful material for replicating metal is Aluminum faced Formica, which after sticking onto MDF can be machined with a router and easily drilled on set. This though cannot be bent around tight corners, so design becomes important.

Drapes:

Drapes are generally hired and come in specific sizes. Large theatre stages had a requirement for drapes and perfected an ideal of drop of 30' (10m). This was generally enough so as not to see over the top yet allowing enough room to raise the drape out of sight of the audience for scene changes. Most large studios have drapes companies on site where all canvases, upholstery and drapes are made. They generally carry a stock of all commonly used materials, plus samples of anything available, and a hire-able stock. All moderate to large feature films have a 'Drapes Person' who will measure and fit any curtains or upholstery required. Drapes come in a wide variety the most common being listed below.

Blackout drapes are the most commonly used, with the best being black velvet. Hired drapes are made with webbing and eyelets around the perimeter through which cord is fixed to enable easy hanging. Standard sizes are 30' x 40', 30' x 30', 30' x 20' or 20'square. Care must be taken to keep the drapes clean on the 'velvet side' during hanging, as cleaning is expensive and laborious. Also, if a drape gets wet it is imperative to dry it prior to storage, as mould and rot soon set in and drapes are expensive to replace (hired drapes are checked on their return). Folding a drape up also requires care so it can be stored correctly (take note how it arrived), the size being written on the back webbing in a specific place and visible when folded. Occasionally you may be asked to cut a hole in a drape to shoot through or rig up something special. The repair charge will be minimal if you restrict your hole to an existing seam as opposed to the middle of the cloth. Always let the hirer know what you have done. If a drape does get dirty it can take an age to clean with a vacuum cleaner. One drape company I knew suggested 'dragging' an open drape across a grass field could be a very effective cleaning method and having tried this, I can only agree.

Velvet drapes also have a 'weft' that changes colour according to the angle it is lit, so repairs have to be carried out with the patch being rotated and aligned prior to fixing, to avoid the repair standing out when hung.

Waterproof blackouts are also available from rigging companies in a heavier material for exterior use.

Chroma key drapes, in green and blue, are another popular choice and the same applies as above for their care and use. Other colours are usually made specifically for the job and are purchased as opposed to hired.

Star Drapes, or cloths, are often used in game shows. These are normal blackout drapes with small light bulbs sewn in and wired to the back. The drapes can be connected together and can be set to light flashing or static. Obvious care is required when hanging these due to the wiring and bulbs, plus of course their extra weight. The traditional, cheaper, and still very effective way to create a star effect is to hang a silver slashed curtain behind an old blackout punctured with holes. When the silver slashed curtain is lit plus a small fan for movement, it reflects through the blackout, making the stars twinkle. Being irregular, this is just like real stars.

Nets and gauze are made up to order and are sometimes referred to as scrim. Gauzes were originally made for theatrical use. They are created from a 30' wide loom and come in various designs in white, grey or black. With these it's possible, with careful use of lighting, to magically change the scene from one to another. Scenic gauze, one of the finer weaves, is most commonly used to create distance or an 'exterior', distant' feel. Sharks-tooth is denser and both types can be either painted or sprayed. When scenic painting, a blackout is required behind the gauze to enable the work to remain visible, and then, when filming, the light source can be changed from the front to the back to achieve the scene changes as described above. Care should be taken to avoid strobing when using multiple gauzes or tracking the camera. It's not normally possible to hire gauzes due to their specific make up, nor to sew them together seamlessly.

Gauzes are also vulnerable to damage when hung and cannot be easily repaired. I once had a thunderous sky painted on a hundred foot gauze ruined by a runner taking a short cut from the pop video being shot on the neighbouring stage. As our large stage door was wide open, the backlight made the gauze virtually invisible from his line of sight and he ran straight through it! An expensive error requiring replacement and a re paint.

Note on Drapes or gauzes: When tying secure at the top, use a bow-knot so it can be easily undone. When wrapping, take them down last, after the stage floor has been swept. You then have room to fold them and keep them on a clean floor.

Sand:

There are various types of sand from builders red to basic fine sand (good for deserts). It can be sold in bags, but is much cheaper by the truckload as the transport is often dearer than the sand. The best way to buy it for scenery is in 1 ton bags (the sort often seen outside building sites) as these bags keep it contained whilst on the stage and can be moved easily with a pallet/forklift truck. Note: have it put on pallets on the stage to aid movement whilst filming. It is possible to alter the colours slightly by using Cementone powdered mortar dye or similar, but this requires the hire of small cement mixer to blend it. Sand is time consuming to lay and move, so try to order and dress the minimum. Painting background scenery can be far more effective than using real sand, as shadows can be painted suggesting larger shapes (dunes). Always lay some old painted canvas on the rostrums or floor prior to dressing with sand otherwise it will disappear through holes and change colour when it dries out. Also, try to avoid making a complete dune out of sand, you will use tons and it won't end up very high, best to build a former first, this will all aid the clear up afterwards.

How Much Do I Need? If building a 20' square set, covering in 2" of dry sand. You'll need 3.7 tons. Dirt, being slightly less dense would need 3.2 tons.

i.e: 1 x cubic foot weighs 0.055 tons approx. (this is for dry sand).

Builders' sand tends to be slightly wet and very much redder in colour, often staining your hands and its surroundings.

Fullers Earth:

This is a very fine, slightly grey material often used for moonscapes or creating dust from car tyres etc. It is basically dried clay and can be harmful if inhaled over a long period. However it is also used as an ingredient in some make-ups and cat litter so is generally safe. Precautions must be allowed for dust so masks should be made available on site whenever it's used for filming.

In my early career I managed to accidently create a simulated nuclear explosion by loading a full and unused bag of fullers on a wooden pallet being used to get gear down from a six storey building in London. It was for a Peter Gabriel Pop Video and the trucks below, with all rear doors opened, had just reversed into an orderly semicircle to collect their gear upon wrap. The bag slipped off the pallet from high up and crash landed resulting in a superb mushroom cloud. This successfully filled every truck that had parked up early! My team was not popular that night, but the visual effect was amazing.

Snow:

There are so many different types of artificial snow that I have listed them in the special effects section later in this book.

Dirt/Topsoil:

Both of these are very heavy and relatively expensive for film sets. With similar attributes to sand, it might be worth considering compost as an alternative as it is a lot less weight and tends to go further (it is a different colour though). I do find that if the compost is mixed with say 'marsh grass' (hired by the clump from film hire specialists) it can be very effective. A common problem with this kind of set is that one usually requires some kind of greenery, such as bushes or trees and it's difficult to hide the pots. So I tend to build these on rostrums built with a gap, allowing for the pot to be concealed. This adds to the cost but is far more aesthetically pleasing.

As with sand, and fullers earth, it can be advantageous to paint the rostrums or stage floor in a base colour of the material, or slightly darker prior to dressing, this will save not only time, but material, when dressing and tidying up.

Trees:

Good greenery hire companies have created special lightweight tree trunks with metal rods protruding allowing for real branches to be attached. This is by far the best method as real trees are too heavy to be practical. The joins between branches and trunk can be easily masked using aerosol insulating foam from your local builders merchant and painted when dry.

Water:

Water, Stage floors and electricity don't mix too well so great care should be taken.

I once tried to do a water tank on the cheap when building a small pond. This was built using thin polythene in multiple layers. Never again. After props, crew, light stands, and even the DOP were working in the pool over a three day shoot, water had leaked through to the bottom of five layers of polythene, shortening my life in the process!

Before dealing with water, check the supply pressure and drainage facility. It may be worth re-positioning all other sets to enable the tank to be near the supply or drain, and to allow for a submersible pump for faster drainage. Flowing water usually requires two tanks, one high up and used for supply from and one to drain into. A pump can then be used between the two to retain levels.

95

A large water tank should be made with a heavy-duty pool liner. These can now be bought from good garden centres, and larger ones can be welded together very quickly up to any size. If one is making a raised pool there are a few things to consider. The weight of the water is such that the tank walls need to be very strong. In fact 1 cubic metre of water weighs 1 ton so bear this in mind for the studio floor loading. I've often found the simplest construction method is either to surround the tank in ladder beams, strapped together as in the following diagram, or to build rostrums around it. Some thin board is worthwhile under the liner to protect it from any unseen sharp items, and also some sand built up in the corners of the tank to prevent the liner being trapped and tearing between walls and floor (see diagram) when filling. Do not fix the liner down until it's filled to avoid tearing it.

Tank liners are usually available in white, blue or black. If creating say a fake mosaic or tiled pool, oil paint stenciled on a white liner can be remarkably effective as the white shows through as the grouting.

It may be necessary to build a spill tank if an invisible horizon is required. This is usually done on just one end of the tank and this needs to be perfectly level. It consists of a separate lower tank built for the overspill. The main liner is taken over the edge and into the spill tank. Care should be taken to make the spill tank large enough, as waves or swimmers generate large volumes of water. Having this too small can be disastrous, especially around the lights.

Waves are created with timber, the longer the timber, straighter the wave. Larger waves can be created with mechanical wave machines, but these are usually used in exterior tanks only due to spillage.

Dust can be a problem in still water tanks. This can be reduced with a tiny drop of washing up liquid dropped in to break up the surface tension just prior to the first shot.

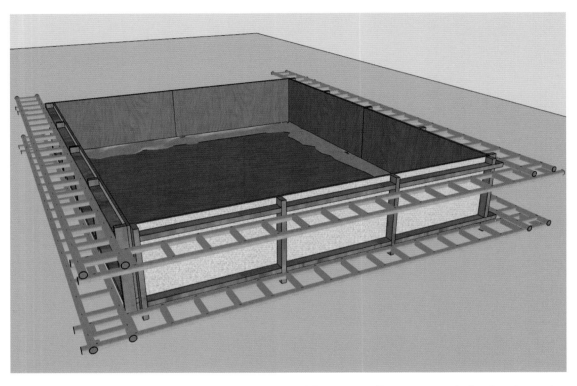

In the tank above, ladder beams are placed horizontally to spread the load on the sides. Also note sand placed loosely in the corners to avoid the liner being trapped in the walls when being filled with water.

A submersible pump is advisable for any tank work (available at Special effects or tool hire companies).

Note: Areas and volumes. 1 x ton of water = 1 cubic metre. Notify the studio if building a water tank, as they may need to notify the authorities for water use. Also make enough allowance for the time taken to fill and drain the tank.

I once had to call the fire brigade to assist in the filling of one of my 20' x 20' tanks as the level was going up at just 1/2" per hour from the studio supply. It would have been the full height one day after it was required!

Rain and other water effects are in the special effects section of this book.

Underwater sets:

Set walls need to be waterproof and are made from sign-writers board known as 'foamex'. This will not expand when wet therefore retaining it's shape, and oil paint is used for colouring. When working in deep tanks qualified divers are required as a precaution. This increases build time, as they can only be underwater for a limited amount of time. This will increase the cost substantially.

Wax:

Wax has some unexpected uses in our industry. When melted it can be poured over water to create very realistic looking and 'breakable' ice. This is especially useful if one is required to heat the water for swimming etc. Melted wax can also be splattered over scenery or wood which, once painted, provides the perfect corroded metal sheet or girders.

Acrylic:

A common material used mainly as a substitute for glass in windows as it's strong, transparent and easily machined. This is sold in various thicknesses and colours, with a full sized sheet usually 2m x 3m (although larger sheets are possible). 6mm is the most common thickness but between 12mm and 20mm is required for supporting actors or crew.

Note: When drilling acrylic, take the edges off the drill bit with a file, to avoid splitting the sheet through heat build-up or, drill very slowly.

Glass:

A standard size for glass is in 8' x 4' sheets and although larger sizes are possible, it becomes difficult to manage. For scenery, laminated or toughened glass should be used. Toughened normally takes a few days to prepare, and is usually made to size. Once sold it cannot be returned, so try to plan disposal at the build stage. Normal thickness for windows is 6mm but anything up to 2" thick is possible for load bearing situations like glass floors, where a strength calculation is made by the glass suppliers depending on span.

Glass is remarkably flexible when new, but can break unexpectedly if brittle and old, like say a rented water tank. So care should be taken when resting on the floor or in a truck. Always support on wooden blocks if possible.

Note: If your set involves many glass sheets, arrange for some handheld 'suckers' and gloves to lift and manhandle. Silicon glue is the preferred method of fixing sheets but time is required for this to set fully (24hrs).

Etched Glass:

Sandblasting glass in a special booth creates etched glass. This again can be time consuming and expensive so a cheaper option may be to use frosted vinyl applied after fitting the glass. Other alternatives include painting glass with wallpaper paste or even using aerosol adhesive through a stencil. This can then be removed with suitable solvents, making it ideal for returning to clear after filming.

Polystyrene:

Commonly used by sculptors this is an extremely light and versatile material. The standard block size is 8' x 4' x 2' and this is cut from a 16' long block. There are various grades available so if sculpting ask for the modelers' fine grade, and check the fire rating (fireproofed is more expensive but is a strict requirement for film sets). Cutting a block can be difficult unless you have a special 'hot wire'. This is an electrical filament connected to a rheostat that heats up the wire to enable cutting. The longer the cutting wire, the more power required. A precise cut can be achieved by rolling the wire over a metal straight edge or a template.

Special adhesive is required for gluing (Evostic 486) or more commonly used aerosol foam glue, often bought with the polystyrene and supplied with a gun. A rough surface is achieved with a wire brush or splattering with acetone. If a rough rock surface is required it's wise to treat the surface afterwards with a few coats Artex or similar (which takes at least overnight to dry) prior to painting, otherwise the paint won't go far or be that long lasting. Coating this way will make it much more hard-wearing. A smooth polystyrene surface is only possible with continuous filling and sanding, which can be time-consuming.

For larger rock faces or moonscapes it's possible to coat the carved surface in a hard setting spray foam which is very durable and hard wearing although the cost can be probative.

Above we see 'Snow White' in advanced stages of being meticulously filled and primed in order to achieve the desired finish. Final model finish with 'Prince Charming' and others is seen to the right on location.

Polystyrene can also be used for more accurate modelling like recreating a 12' long sweet cup above, plus of course the sweets inside. The specially designed label was printed onto canvas and wrapped around.

A giant hamburger, prior to completion, created entirely out of polystyrene for a well-known burger chain.

Plaster:

Plastering is a specialist trade within the film industry. Being water based, quick drying and infinitely adaptable, it is one of the cheapest methods to provide very effective repeat exterior finishes. A simple mould can be created of virtually any exterior surface like brick or stonework, even tree bark. Most large studio complexes have their own plaster shops and provide a chart of regularly used moulds. An ideal use may be to replicate a particular surface shot on location to a stage set built to match for continuity.

Special considerations need to be observed when buying plaster sheets. Pouring wet plaster into the mould creates the sheets, and usually Hessian is laid in the wet plaster to 'hold' it together for strength whilst maneuvering. Once dry, the sheets are stapled to the flattage and the sheet joins are repaired with more wet plaster and a trowel. As a result one usually is offered two prices, to supply 'sheets only' or 'fitted sheets', with the joints repaired, the latter being more expensive. It is advisable to use older flats as a base for any plasterwork, as stapling and trimming knives are used to fit the sheets and these can leave scratches and protruding staples, therefore damaging the flats.

Once fitted, the sheets require sealing and painting, which is usually done by painters using shellac followed by a base coat. Due to drying times, a minimum of two days should be allowed for this process, but the results are well worth it as it's far more realistic than vacuum formed sheets. Bear in mind that finished plaster sheets on flattage do become very heavy, so movement once completed can be an issue.

Vacuum Forming:

This process, like plastering, involves melting a plastic sheet over a glassfibre mould and 'sucking' the air out. Once cooled the plastic remains in this shape. This process is repeated to produce many identical sheets, which can be applied to the flats. One standard sheet tends to be smaller than a standard 8' x 4' and the designs generally flow in a horizontal direction. The natural colour of this material is grey although it is also available in clear or white, the clear being especially good for ice effects. You can also get the stronger and more fire retardant 'ABS'. Although extremely quick it is difficult to hide the joins with pvc, and stone and brickwork are often left with 'hollows' identifying it as plastic as opposed to the real thing.

Glass Fibre:

Similar to plaster and vacuum formed pvc this is created in a mould, It is far more suitable for long term use in places such as theme parks and exhibitions as it can be pre-coloured and fireproofed. It is much stronger and more resilient to the weather, but cost can be an issue for filming purposes.

Most film plaster specialists can supply brochures showing all available moulds. Plaster specialists can be found in most of the major studios plus of course the usual industry publications mentioned earlier in this book. Note that you should always specify 'fireproof' when ordering anything used for filming or exhibition purposes.

PAINT

'Anyone can paint' is a term all too frequently used in the film industry when trying to cut labour costs, and to delegate to runners or production assistants. However, it is not until a skilled painter is seen graining a pine door or introducing a damp patch on a ceiling that their skills become apparent, and an important complement to any good art department.

As an art director painting is generally contracted out to a specialist. However there have been and still will be many occasions where, because of time or money, we need to get down and do it ourselves, or we have to understand the technique well enough to explain to an impatient producer how long the process will take. One also has to deal with the paint suppliers, as paint needs ordering prior to painters being contracted. *I once telephoned through a Pantone reference number to a paint supplier who claimed to be able to match any colour requested. When I arrived on set to see pink, instead of red, I was not best pleased. The suppliers' pantone chart had been hung on a wall in their shop for over six months and had faded in the sun. Though the number was correct they kindly decided to forego the six hundred pound paint bill!*

The remarkable thing about painting scenery is that it can easily deceive and indeed, this is one of the reasons why I wanted to pursue film as a career. Paint is the most important material to enable this, and I am often surprised at how little the medium is utilized to its fullest extent.

I must admit to being initially surprised when seeing a painter start a project in seemingly the wrong colour, then walk off for a break while it dries. It is only when you see the final top colour and treatment that you realize what his intention was in the first place. Painters' skills have been learnt through apprenticeships from an earlier era and are only occasionally passed on.

It's also worth noting that too much work on certain effects can be detrimental. I once was attempting to paint some vacuum formed stonework and got very carried away doing 'dark in the hollows' and 'light on the peaks' in all the right colours but the final result looked very flat and theatrical. It was far too overworked, I might as well not have bothered with the vacuum formed sheets in the first instance!

Paint brings scenery alive, and if used correctly, can save thousands off the budget. Water-based mediums are preferred due to drying times being quicker. However an occasional mix with oil paint or spirit based paints can have marvelous results when creating marble and similar effects.

There are many books available on the techniques involved which describe the subject in far greater detail than I can do in one chapter, but virtually all are for permanent results. Film painters often use shortcuts, due to time and budgetary constraints, and this is the specific area I will attempt to cover. These techniques are not designed to last, but are more than adequate for short term use and filming. A selection of progression photos concludes this chapter.

Laying In/ Priming:

As with all painting, the finished surface is dependent upon the material to be painted, so time spent filling and sanding is well spent for a good overall effect. A chemically cured filler (like a car filler) is often better than water based as it has a quicker drying time, and is a lot more durable and easier to sand down. It is common for the scenery to be moved and transported once painted, and water based fillers tend to crack and fall out when scenery is manhandled.

Sheet materials have been transformed with the use of MDF (medium density fibreboard) owing to its ease of cutting and smooth surface. However, this is usually fixed with pins, screws or nails all of which require initial filling, essential for high gloss finishes.

Newly painted canvas, for say cycloramas or ceiling pieces requires priming, usually in white, prior to scenic work or top coat. This should ideally be undertaken with a brush or large roller to flatten the 'weft' otherwise the cloth will dry patchy, due to the canvas strands drying inconsistently. Spray guns or 'Airless sprayers' should only be used over a pre-primed canvas for the same reason.

If painting plasterwork, or PVC, it should be coated in a shellac varnish often known as 'Button Polish' which though smelly, will dry quickly and act as a good bonding coat for any water-based paints. This is useful for preventing stains (like coffee cup rings which seep through the topcoats on studio floors etc.) and good for painting onto newly cut paper stencils as it prevents the paint being absorbed into the paper, therefore extending its life.

Painted Finishes for film and TV:

To give the look of rare and expensive wood i.e. oak, mahogany or teak to inexpensive materials such as plywood or pine.

Techniques and colours:

The main technique is to apply the chosen base colour (suggestions in tables to follow) and allow it to dry. Remember that emulsion paint generally dries lighter in tone as opposed to when wet.

Next seal this with a clear acrylic varnish and allow to dry.

This sealed base colour is now ready to be worked in the graining colour, or 'scumble' which is mixed into a different colour for each type of wood.

Scumble is translucent and slow drying to allow time to create the effects. This can be purchased as a clear liquid from all good paint stores, then coloured with your choice of pigment or stainer.

Apply the scumble over the prepared base by brushing evenly in the direction of

107

the grain. Next use a graining comb or rocker (from all high quality paint suppliers) to brush through the 'still wet' scumble. The rubber comb leaves the grain lines, and the rocker creates the knots in the grain. From here it can be over grained with another weak scumble mix to deepen the effect, or patted with a cloth to soften it. When dry this can be sealed with glaze or wax. It is possible to buy metal combs which give an assortment of grains if required, but that's for serious painters.

Scumble is often used in paint effects acting as a drying retardant to allow for working the paint.

Colour palette to below for the most common woods:

Wood Type	Base Colour	Seal in	Top Colour
Mahogany	Red Oxide	Gloss Acrylic Glaze	Vandyke Brown/ Scumble fine grain.
Oak	Yellow Ochre	Matt Acrylic Glaze	Medium Brown/ Scumble knotty grain.
Beech	Medium Cream	Matt Acrylic Glaze	Medium Brown/ Scumble fine graining
Pine	Pale Cream	Matt Acrylic Glaze	Light Brown/ Scumble knotty grain.

Always try to find a reference of the chosen wood prior to finalizing the colour choice.

Once complete this could be 'Lime washed' by applying a very thin coat of 'watered down' white paint.

Marbling: Choose a reference of the desired marble (this will dictate the colour palette)

Apply base colour and allow to dry. Seal this with acrylic varnish.

Make a weak scumble mix of the desired top colour and apply evenly over the surface.

Use a scrunched up plastic bag to 'pat' the scumble and continue 'working' this over the whole surface. It should now resemble marble.

Additionally, splatter with methylated spirit to disperse the newly applied scumble to create a slightly different marble design.

Colour palette to below for the most common marbles:

Marble Type	Base Colour	Seal in	Top Colour
Carrara	White	Gloss Acrylic Glaze	Various Greys/ Scumble mix applied with plastic bag or rag.
Sienna	Yellow Ochre	Gloss Acrylic Glaze	Black/Scumble mix and Burnt Sienna applied with plastic bag or rag.
Malachite	Deep Green	Gloss Acrylic Glaze	Black then White applied with plastic bag or rag.

Finally, draw in 'veins' over the design with either a fine brush or bird feather. Once satisfied, let it dry and apply a final coat of varnish to seal in.

Another effective marbling technique is to create it on lining paper and when dry, paste direct onto the walls. This is especially useful for large sets where consistency is important and where the individual slabs require definition. The width of the paper becomes the width of the slab avoiding time-consuming 'lining' in stones when dry.

The basic technique involves making a low flat tank (to fit a workable sized piece of paper). Lining with polythene and filling with water (the paper colour being the base colour, which could be pre painted) then pouring various colour of oil paint in and swirling it around. Being oil paint it will float on top. Then the paper is unrolled and slid under the water. When the paper is pulled out, the oil paint sticks to it resembling marble. Once dry this can be pasted on to the flattage and then sealed if required to achieve a shine.

Rag rolling and stippling:

These are popular techniques for breaking up large surfaces. They were very popular in the past, giving remarkably attractive finishes despite their simplicity to create. Many very expensive types of wallpaper resemble this finish which can be extremely subtle, depending on colour choice.

Start with a base colour of choice, next mix either a variation of this colour (or any other top colour) and pour onto a small board. Tear some soft rag (about 60cm sq) and roll into a bundle to 'roll over' the paint on the board (gloves are a good idea here). Do this several times until the rag is fully soaked and roll this on another spare board to dry the cloth a little, then test the result. When happy, transfer your wet painted rag bundle to the desired wall and start rolling up (the wall), this can be repeated several times before re-charging and is quite a quick process. Make sure you remain consistent with your design and re-roll as necessary to fill in the gaps. This could be repeated with a third colour but two are usually adequate.

Different designs can be created with different rags and even polythene bags wrapped around paint rollers are remarkably effective.

Stippling is a variation on this technique and requires a 'box brush' or a low-pressure spray gun with wide jet over the base coat. For very large areas a special stipple gun can be hired from paint suppliers.

The top 'stipple' colour is usually quite a wet mix and could be various colours, if spraying, start high and work slowly down the walls to avoid dripping.

Graduation:

A smooth mix between dark and light colours. A scenic artist usually undertakes this as though it may be simple to look at, it can be difficult to perfect. It is best used to simulate sky with the pale colour closest to the bottom.

The most straightforward method is to mix a minimum of three colours, the darkest, a middle and the lightest. Paint these in horizontal bands, the widest being the top band, then allow to dry. Next, using a spray gun, spray the second colour down into the top colour (always work from the top). Once satisfied with this, re mix your paint to the lighter colour and spray the lower band into the middle band. The more horizontal coloured bands used, the better the graduation. Always spray into the band above to prevent dripping paint damaging the already sprayed surface, as touching up any errors can be difficult. I also find that setting the spray gun to a 'low' pressure thus providing a 'dottle' is far more effective and easier to control. A higher pressure will create unwanted 'clouds' which can't be seen in closeup but looks uneven when viewed from afar.

Textured Surfaces:

Old weathered surfaces can be created on MDF and Plywood by mixing ground chalk or calcium carbonate with paint. This thickens the paint considerably providing a good key for base and subsequent coats. A watery wash of black and raw umber over the top coat gives the appearance of age which can be built up in the corners etc. with a sponge. When first applied it can appear quite drastic but will usually dry a lot softer in tone. Dabbing with a sponge in a raw umber/black mix, gives the impression of rising damp.

Another effective technique for replicating the texture of flat stone rendering (like an exterior wall) might be to coat in Artex or wallpaper in standard woodchip paper used back to front.

Brick PVC Sheets:

Painting colours vary according to brick type, but for standard red brick prime with a red oxide emulsion. When dry, mix three other colours using your red oxide base, say red and black, and red and burnt umber. With a small roller, separate colours can be used to pick out the occasional brick in a random pattern. The mortar colour is made by mixing yellow ochre, white and raw umber and looks best painted with a small fitch (paint brush) once all is dry. All the above will require ageing down with water, black and raw umber. Put the neat paint on first, then wash it down with water.

For London stock (the yellow type of brick) use yellow ochre, white and burnt umber instead of the red oxide above and age as above.

Rocks and Stonework:

We are often asked to reproduce specific rocks (from a location) in a studio and these are usually done either in carved polystyrene, plaster or PVC sheets. A good reference of the actual rock is essential here to replicate and identify the base colour required. With carved polystyrene the initial finish (base) should be coated in Artex or similar, to aid drying and make the rock more hard wearing. Once a base colour has been applied, use a watered down black, white and raw umber to provide the lighter/darker highlights. This can be done with a very 'dry' brush accentuating the texture then finally aged down with a watery umber. A final touch of 'Lichen' can be made by mixing neat yellow ochre with sawdust in a small bucket. Make a 'porridgy' mix, then pick up globules by hand and throw it on the rocks. Use Brunswick green with sawdust in the technique above for a realistic moss alternative.

Blocking:

The process is started by painting the surface normally at first, sealing with glaze then ageing with raw umber and a black mix, this diluted with water and applied by brush before rubbing with a soft rag.

Blocking is used in heavily worn areas and has the impression of revealing the wood underneath the paint. A short piece of wood is dipped into a yellow ochre and umber paint mix then 'scraped or tapped' quickly across areas needing to look heavily worn. This effectively puts the wood colour back on the top coat, but just in the areas that would realistically wear - a bit like a complete reverse of what might be expected. The eye is deceived into thinking that this is normal wear and tear, but be careful not to overuse this technique, as 'less' is often 'more' in this case.

Liquid Bitumen:

This is good for making a set look tired or nicitine stained which is perfect for styling old rooms and pubs. Be aware of it's strong odour when applying roughly with a brush and wiping with a rag, but it will give great results.

The door is aged around all areas of normal wear and tear with a watery mix of raw umber and black, then dabbed with a rag prior to blocking.

A combination of ageing and 'blocking' can be extremely effective for achieving that 'lived in' feel. A small piece of wood is coated in bare wood colour (yellow ochre and raw umber mix) and carefully 'touched' on the edges that would normally wear.

Colour image progressions showing painting techniques for wood, marble, brick and stonework surfaces are on the following three pages.

Mahogany:

Red oxide is used as a base coat, followed by acrylic sealer.

Allow for the surface to dry. Make a 50/50 mix of burnt umber and scumble.

Paint inside the panels first using the scumble mix. Use your brush or fine graining comb to create the grain effect.

Once happy with the panels, coat the remaining door and soften all with a soft dry brush.

When dry, seal with another coat of clear acrylic sealer.

Pine:

Pale cream is the preferred base colour followed by a coat of acrylic sealer.

Start with panels and grain as you go with yellow ochre/ black and scumble mix. A rubber 'rocker' is used for the knots.

Complete the panels and mouldings, followed by the stiles and rails.

Soften all the grain with the brush while still wet until satisfied.

Allow to dry before sealing with Matt Acrylic Sealer.

Carrara Marble:

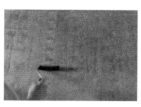

Apply a watery dark grey/scumble over a sealed pale grey.

Splatter with methylated spirit to breakup the surface.

Soften the effect by stroking with a soft dry brush.

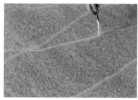

When nearly dry apply graining with a brush or feather.

Soften more with a soft roller and allow to dry. Seal with acrylic sealer.

Malachite Marble:

Apply a black scumble mix with a rag over a dark green base.

Soften the effect with a clean rag until satisfied.

Dip a clean rag into some white and 'dab' onto surface.

Soften this whilst still wet.

Paint grains with a brush or feather and seal with gloss acrylic sealer.

Brickwork:

Seal surface with shellac and lay in with preferred mortar colour.

Use red oxide/ burnt umber colour for bricks and apply with a short haired roller.

Pick out some individual bricks in darker and lighter shades.

An overall wash with a watery raw umber creates overall ageing.

The completed brickwork once dry.

Stonework:

Seal original surface with shellac and lay in dark grey shadow colour.

Pick out some areas in a lighter colour and some with darker tones with a dry brush.

When dry, wash down with a watery raw umber.

Mix some sawdust with neat yellow ochre in a bucket. Flick this, by hand onto the surface for Lichen effect.

The rock surface when dry.

117

ARCHITECTURE

Basic Architecture:

 Many books have been written on architecture, so I would recommend individual research as and when required depending on the brief. Here I have decided to treat the different periods in a very simplistic way. By no means should it be taken as exact reference material, but merely as a guide for quick reference to be followed by more thorough research. One of the most important attributes of a good designer is to be able to look at a style and differentiate which details make it look a specific period. Incorporating the correct colours, details and, above all, proportions will give the set a period regardless of the material used to construct it. Another important key is to bear in mind that local buildings tend to be built from local materials, as can be seen all around the world. Therefore if the local sand is red, as in many parts of Africa, the local architecture will reflect this. A stone cottage based in the Cotswolds' UK will be build from local grey Cotswold stone.

Periods:

Ancient Egypt 3000 BC - 900 BC. Self explanatory really, Pyramids and stuff!

Classical 850 BC - 450 AD. Here think ancient Greece and temples. (Ref. Parthenon Greece).

Roman 44 BC - 500 AD. Heavily influenced by the earlier Greek period using decorative Ionic and Corinthian columns. The Romans cleverly invented concrete, which resulted in larger arches, vaults and domes. (Ref. Coliseum, Rome, Italy).

Typical fluted column tops above: Left to right, Ionic, Corinthian and Doric.

Gothic 1100 - 1500. Pointed arches and elaborate stonework influenced buy Moorish architecture in Spain. It was found that the walls could be thinner using these arches yet be strong enough to support more decorative carved elements like Gargoyles.

Renaissance 1400 - 1600. More symmetry than earlier periods with regard to the doors and windows but shows a revival of the more classical columns and pilasters.

Baroque 1600 - 1830. More elaborate than Renaissance with twisted columns and decorative stonework. Think the Palace of Versailles (France) here.

Rococo 1650 - 1790. Think elaborate scrolls and curves and more intricate patterns together with pastel shades (Ref. Prague Castle, Czech Republic).

Neo Classical 1730 - 1925. Tall columns and domed roofs, very symmetrical, think The White House (USA).

Art Nouveau 1890 - 1914. Originating in France this was a much looser style incorporating slender curves and decorations. Basically a rebellion against the earlier periods, creating smoother shapes, and often using stained glass and mosaics.

Art Deco 1925 - 1937. More complex and decorative shapes with many curves and cubic forms incorporated with a very strong sense of line. Often terraced with zigzag shapes and bands of colour.

The Period House:

Classical Style 1666 - 1710. Much of London was rebuilt following the great fire in the Classical Style with primary examples being Covent Garden Piazza and the newly rebuilt St. Paul's Cathedral (in London). Being influenced by early Greek, Italian and French architecture it basically copied the much earlier styles above. The following pages show some basic examples of UK architecture through the periods.

Medieval Streets.

Note here: Non-symmetry, overhanging eves, timber frames and thatched roofs. The streets were generally narrower than today allowing for foot traffic only.

Medieval Interiors.

121

Georgian 1710 - 1810.

Note Here: Symmetrical proportions, large central doorways and larger windows that were designed, prior to commercial electric power to allow for more light.

Georgian Interiors.

Note: Wood panelling, large fire surrounds, wooden window shutters. Heavy large shaped mouldings giving more of a sense of 'grandeur'.

Late Victorian 1875 - 1899.

Victorian Interiors.

Note: Ornate decorations, heavy mouldings and dark wood furnishings.

1930s and 1960s Architecture.

1930 and 1960's Interiors.

Note: The 30's overall had more curves and sweeping lines. 60's, more metal, concrete and plastic surfaces.

Summarising, the most important features to consider are ceiling height, mouldings, window size and design, together with overall proportions of the building.

As a conclusion I can recommend the book 'The English Home' by Doreen Yarwood published by Batsford for further research in many of the above periods. Stylists often consider this the industry standard research book in the UK.

LANDSCAPES

Creating Landscapes:

 Landscapes can quite obviously cover a vast array of alternatives, so research or a photo reference, is always the best place to start. There are some basic rules of perspective (covered later in this book) that need to be followed in order to achieve anything realistic. The most important of these by far being the horizon height. Even where no horizon is visible, this rule should be followed.

In order to achieve ultimate distance the horizon height should be the at a similar height to the camera. Anything other than this and your set will look like a set, as opposed to an attempt at reality.

The easiest way to achieve this is simply to paint it on the cyc, if available, or alternatively, paint, or rent a backdrop. The latter can reduce many of the lighting options for the DOP as the sky and land are effectively on the same plane, making it difficult to adjust the light independently. That effectively puts more emphasis on the scenic artist's talents. There will be a noticeable difference of colour between the floor and painted cyc. This is because the light reflects from vertical planes differently to horizontal planes. Add to this the complications of hiding plant pots or roots against the backing, and you'll soon wish you'd built the whole thing on a rostrum, ideally a ramp, getting seamlessly from floor level up to horizon height.

I find the most visually accurate and cost effective method is to separate all the elements within a ramp, as below.

The foreground floor can be on the stage floor, allowing safety or the actors. A small ramp can lead the eye up to the next raked rostrum, the back of which can be easily accessed and dressed (potted plants can be placed between the rostrums therefore hiding the pots). Together with the next raked rostrum, this could be where the dressing could be reduced in scale, enhancing the perspective effect. The final or horizon can then be painted on the cyc. This allows for access and lighting, without damaging the set dressing. If required, one can achieve more 'distant atmosphere' by hanging a grey 'scenic gauze' at the last ramp accentuating the perspective.

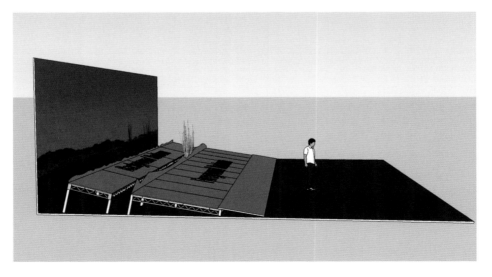

A perspective landscape built on two separate rostrums viewed from the side.

Here the same set as seen from the front obscuring all the access and lighting channels. The same technique can be used for a multitude of scenarios.

Ramping the floor up to the horizon enhances the diminished scale here. The moon, created by a single lamp on a stand covered in a black drape, is behind a gauze. This gauze has been sprayed with a horizon mist and some clouds to complete the effect. The stars were created by cutting up a roll of 3M's silver foil into 1/2" squares and sticking onto the black drape. To enhance the effect one needs about double the quantity one would expect, these then have the appearance of twinkling when seen through the gauze.

In the picture above: The background mountains are painted together with a cut out foreground peninsular on the left. The water, done again on a ramp was a black board with food wrap stretched over, remarkably cheap yet very effective. The foreground waves were individually made in food wrap and then laid on top. The use of scenic artwork can greatly enhance the impression of distance as atmosphere can be lightly sprayed over the original painting. Usually the palest sky colour is used in for this effect.

Forests and Jungles:

There is a common misconception that green is the best place to start when designing a jungle or forest set. In reality very little light gets into rainforests, and one is often better off starting with black as a base colour for the scene. This would then have the effect of enhancing any light, paint or greenery used. Renting large plants can be expensive so it's wise to use as much scenic artist work as possible (see scenic artwork later in this book). Also as trees are generally big and tall, one sees the trunks, but the branches are often a lot higher than eye level and it's these that create the light-reducing canopy. This canopy can sometimes be seen in the far distance, and if so, can be scenic painted thus avoiding hiring large trees.

Greenery hire companies sometimes have a supply of large pre-carved polystyrene tree trunks that are an ideal starting point, as real trunks are far too heavy or too skinny for a large forest, plus real ones come in a large pot requiring dressing out. Just a couple of large fake trunks can set the whole thing off with the rest of the trunks being done with simple 2 dimensional cut outs. Prior to all of this though, you should hang all the top branches in the studio rig. This task is made much easier with a clear floor space, and once hung, the set can be roughed in, first with the trunks, and then with the hired greenery. Building the set on a rostrum again helps as it enables one to hide the plants' pots through the rostrum floor. However, just tipping plants on their sides is also fairly effective, though the plants don't like it. If plants are real it may be worth renting 'grow lights' to keep them alive during the build, and of course, don't forget to water them!

131

Above: The scale of this forest is achieved through the use of a few large tree trunks. These can be relatively simply made as eventually they will be dressed with ivy and moss covering any faults. If one first hangs the overhead branches, it allows more working space prior to the ground and plant dressing. A gauze has been used in the background with light rays carefully sprayed on between the trees.

Fields and grass:

Grass is hard to replicate with a short build time and I would recommend using the real stuff as opposed to anything fake, even though the fake is improving greatly. Marsh grass is fairly straightforward and available to purchase in 'clumps', which can be easily dressed in. If this is initially laid onto polythene it retains moisture and makes tidying up easier. Real turf can be purchased on a soil free roll now although I tend to prefer the separate sods as they can be dressed around tree trunks and plants more easily for realism. Try to allow time for the grass to settle and consider getting grow lights, and possibly a fan, to keep the air moving. In as little as 24hrs this should start recovering and look quite effective. *I once built a set for some stills using real grass and it grew so much over the two-week period we actually had to mow it!* If flowers are required I would recommend using fake ones as they look great and are very resilient to abuse.

Long established grass like hay or crops can present their own set of problems in a studio. Once I created a corn field and not only had the dilemma of where to source the corn (it was as usual out of season) but how, once sourced, to stand it up on a stage as if it were growing. It was sourced with the help of a farmer who suggested I might try 'thatching reed' which was being stored in a barn located just 2 hours' drive from the studio. I bought the whole stock for that year! When dressing in, we sandwiched the reed between thin plywood strips at its base, and stapled the strips together giving us 8' long 'runs' of standing reed. These were then supported with timber on the floor giving us the impression of it growing, see photo below;

The loose reed is laid out onto a rostrum and the stalks sandwiched between two thin pieces of plywood. Once stapled together it can be stood upright and braced.

Here the thatching reed is initially laid out flat on a rostrum top, measured to a consistent hieght, then sandwiched between strips of plywood. Once the strips are stapled to each other and trimmed, it's possible to stand them up vertically and dress them into the set.

In the background the scenic artist is working on the clouds in the sky prior to painting the landscape below. When lit, the painted landscape should merge with the real set as in the photo overleaf. The perspective effect can be greatly enhanced by carefully graduating the blue sky colour.

The finished set with the strips of finished reed leading up to the scenic backdrop. The large shape above was supposed to be the underside of a spaceship hovering close by.

Deserts:

There are numerous different types of desert, and generally the same perspective rules apply from earlier in this chapter. Sand is a relatively cheap material but moving it is expensive. As a result your design would benefit from some alternative method to create sand dunes. Sand, being wind blown, creates some amazing real life shapes especially when seen in the distance, and this can be hard to replicate with scenery. When ordering sand, specify 'dry' as the usual wet builders sand never dries out properly, and it also changes colour as it dries. I've found it cheapest bought loose in 1 x ton sacks. These can stay on stage close to where it's needed.

For sand dunes, I once experimented with plywood formers profiled on the ridge and base, wrapped and stapled with canvas. Once painted, these stretched perfectly into attractive concave shapes providing very effective dunes. However the overall size was restricted as one needed to paint the canvas without treading on it. This method saved huge amounts of sand, as it was only needed for top dressing. Sharks tooth gauze is another possible material as it's very stretchy providing a similar result, but the formers become slightly visible and any marks inside will show up.

Simple, cheap and light, once covered in canvas or gauze, then painted, it can make very effective distant sand dunes.

Other, more traditional methods for creating dunes involve polystyrene carving, and solid wood with formers and cladding in plaster or sprayed composites etc. The latter method is very labour intensive, but makes it suitable for walking on over high areas. Ripples can be achieved last thing with a specially made wooden rake. It is claimed that ripples can be achieved by leaving a fan running overnight but I'm sceptical here because of its reach, and the fact that someone will inevitably walk over it the following morning, negating the whole effect. It's a good method for small areas though.

MODELS AND PERSPECTIVE

Models are used extensively in our industry due to cost and practicality and one of the most important considerations here is scale.

Walls, windows and doors can be built virtually any size. However practical lighting elements, and other dressing can be very tricky unless carefully considered. As a result, it's wise to source as many of these details as possible prior to deciding the overall scale of the model.

Models involving cars should generally be at a pre-defined scale linked to vehicles that already exist in the shops. There is also a vast array of materials available from specialist architectural model-making suppliers, such as columns and brickwork, however these tend to be quite expensive. Most repeat elements can be moulded fairly quickly using fast-cast and easier still now with the use of 3d printers, the latter being superb for elements that require left and right hand versions, as the initial design can be easily flipped with compatible software.

If one is building a model to match part of a full sized set, it's wise to design both together at full scale, then reduce this finished design to form the model drawings.

This is a fairly straightforward process thanks in part to CAD. Both model and full scale set may not appear exactly similar when filming, but this is sometimes due to the different camera lens characteristics.

It's also worth bearing in mind that building a model 'larger in size' will not necessarily make it better, it is better to keep it to a manageable size for working on and provide lighting access.

Note. If designing exterior building models, in daytime, the windows always tend to look better if they are blacked out behind the glass, the possibility of curtains or blinds should be sufficient for a realistic effect. If the reflection of the sky is required, use a blue reflector behind the camera.

Here the scale of the model interior was dictated by the practical light bulbs on all the columns. The model ship was suspended on cable to drop down into shot.

139

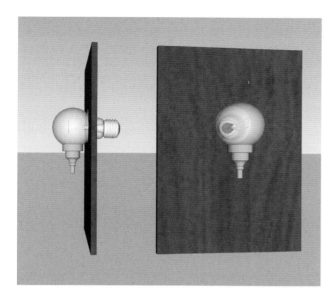

This detail of the previous model shows the actual light bulbs, which were fixed through the model columns into their socket behind, with the decorative elements later glued onto the bulb base (with heat resistant glue). This gives the appearance of a larger light. One's scale is restricted due to available light bulb sizes.

This model bus was constructed using the front end of an existing American truck. The new back end was built from scratch; windows, seats and luggage. By using the complicated front end from another existing model, build time was reduced.

The completed bus on set. The desert needs to be built proportional to the scale of the bus, including the road, gravel, backing and greenery.

Water doesn't scale down very well and if doing model boats, there is a limit as to how small one can build them. Shooting at high speed, therefore slowing down the wave motion and making it more realistic can sometimes overcome this.

In the model street wet down below, aerosol spay oil was applied to make it look damp, this avoids the whole area drying out too quickly under the lights and helps continuity whilst filming.

A model street with a wet effect road done with aerosol oil. This can be helpful as water dries out quickly under the lights.

If filming water with architecture and furniture, it may be worth considering doing the surroundings as a scaled model, then shooting the full sized furniture and water, separately for later addition. This is because the water scales better if shot real size and furniture can be expensive and time consuming to replicate as a model, whereas relatively cheap to hire for real.

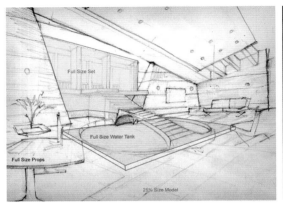

The above preliminary sketch shows which elements are filmed 'real size' and which are models. The completed model is on the right, less furniture.

If filmed from a motion control rig, it's even possible to move the camera in shot. This move can then be replicated and scaled on the camera rig. When all is composited together, the furniture will look as though it's inside the model. One does need a pre-defined scale to achieve this successfully and a trustworthy camera crew.

The props here are shot seperately against black from a motion control rig. Adequate stage space is essential when filming the full sized props though. The model camera move above will dictate the scaled shooting distance from the full sized props left.

143

Perspective:

The use of forced perspective can have an incredibly rewarding effect on camera, whether in models or full sized sets and often attracts attention. Cost can be very prohibitive though, certainly with architecture, as all the mouldings need to be specially made and if the camera moves too much, it can reveal the illusion. It is primarily for this reason that perspective models are more popular for theatre sets as opposed to film. Exaggerated perspective has been used in the set below for a bank commercial.

The general rule to achieve distance is to create a vanishing point at a similar height as the viewer or camera, with every horizontal disappearing to that point. This includes the floor height. There are many rules with perspective but one of the most common must be the even spacing of columns or uprights receding away from camera. This can be solved at the design stage by using the simple method below.

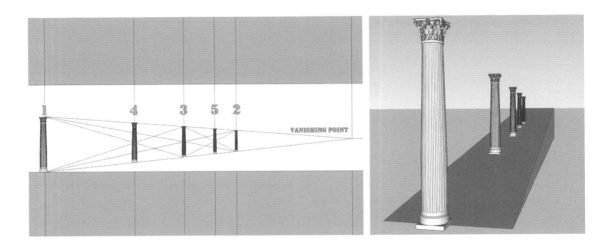

If one draws the columns in the numerical order 1 – 5, then joining the top to bottom diagonals gives you a position the column in between, and an accurate height. This can then be repeated for the other middle columns and can be used in numerous ways to create the perspective effect in a fast and efficient way.

145

The sketch above shows an unusually 'high' vanishing point because it's supposed to be viewed from first floor window, looking down at the houses outside.

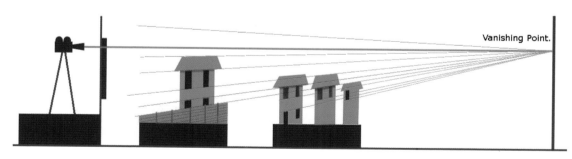

Vanishing Point.

Looking at the same design in elevation, the house roofs appear to rise up towards the vanishing point yet are built on level rostrums. As a result the rostrums, in blue, will have the effect of the going downhill. As can be seen in the next photo.

146

Here the shot seen from the camera POV shows how deceptive perspective can be. All the houses and fences, were built as in the previous elevation, with their horizontals aligning to the vanishing point, yet the rostrums or road appeared to go downhill, were actually level.

SCENIC ARTWORK AND PHOTO-BACKINGS

 The rapid advance of large format printing and postproduction techniques has had a dramatic effect on our industry and reduced demand for the more traditional scenic artwork. Photo-backing companies usually carry a large stock of existing images from previous jobs and are also able to photograph and manipulate anything desired. It's worth allowing for some basic retouching in your budget, plus delivery of the backing. The image, when printed, will usually be very large and the original photo should be taken from a 10" x 8" plate camera ideally as opposed to digital.

Real painting still retains many advantages though. A skilled scenic artist can transform a set in as little as a day, and can paint exactly what is required as opposed to 'making do' with the only available photo. A photo blow-up may still require re-touching and photographer rights need to be paid prior to use, even if just a view through a window. More than likely we will be asked to create a 'non recognizable' or 'arbitrary' cityscape, and virtually every photo can be recognized as being in an actual location. A 35mm still may look fantastic in its original format, but multiply the scale upwards 100 fold and it could reveal many faults. Uprights are one of the major concerns, as the original image will have lens distortion, especially near the edges, this will be noticeable if seen through window bars or upright columns on set. Some of this can be corrected at extra cost but this is hard to budget for. Also, basic elements like 'horizon height' can be difficult to establish prior to building the set and printing the backing. These errors are expensive to rectify on a pre-light day!

A photograph may contain notable landmarks and be low on definition when blown up to the required size. Note here the buildings on the right are leaning outwards due to camera lens distortion. This can be corrected, but at extra cost.

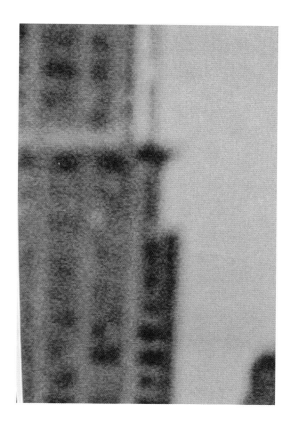

A close-up of the same image reveals very distorted uprights and lack of resolution in the original. This sample was especially printed at actual scale required. Unless another image can be found one may be better off having it painted.

In a scenic painted backdrop, above, you get what you want in just a few days as above from an experienced scenic artist. This backing took just three days to paint.

Scenic artists are specialists and as such it's wise to prepare the set to enable him/her to work as efficiently as possible. References should have been discussed earlier and if possible the backing, or cyclorama, should be primed, dry, and in the correct colour. This usually depends on the subject matter, but generally the darkest colour in the sky will be a good starting point. The artist usually starts from the top (to avoid splashes) and paints the shadow colours before building to the mid colours and highlights. Lights and access are also important so make sure the set is clear and some light is at hand. They will also need to know the ideal camera height to establish where to put the horizon. Overall, a painted scenic backing will cost you more than a photo blowup but will possibly give you more satisfaction in knowing everything will look right on the day.

If planning a photo blow-up make sure your scale is correct by accurately measuring the largest elements in the photo with reality in your set. Try also to get a 'full size' sample printed so as to see the finished definition as seen earlier.

I once had a general office background blown up and on arrival the rear of the printed computer monitors on my image were far too large a scale. Fortunately I could lower the backing to obscure them.

SPECIAL EFFECTS

Special effects (SFX) generally cover atmospherics, pyrotechnics, animatronics (models that require mechanical movement) and many mechanical rigs that could carry potential danger unless operated by a specially trained technician. It's long winded but if in any doubt, consult a specialist company or supervisor.

There are many effects companies and these usually, like prop houses specialise in various areas of expertise.

When getting a quotation, you will need to know the location area, as transport and fuel will be added, and a good idea of the effect required. The technicians are generally in-house, but set rates are charged for overtime, mileage and expenses to and from location. They usually carry a full kit of spares and these costs can often be outweighed by peace of mind when filming.

As a general rule of thumb; anything that you feel unsure about, you should seek advice as you can be sure that the effect has been done successfully in the past by someone in the industry.

If filming rain or snow effects a constant water supply makes life easier and a fireman's hydrant or a manhole and standpipe can usually be accessed (with water authority permission) on most streets. Failing this, a portable bowser should be sought.

A Fire Hydrant access cover and adjacent sign, look for this on your recce if water effects are required.

A cheaper route may be to access a neighbours' own supply (remember to bring an assortment of hose attachments though).

There are various straightforward effects that can be achieved by the art department by simply dry hiring the correct kit and below is a list of various items that could be useful to any movie.

Smoke:

There are different machines and devices to achieve different types of smoke. Things to consider are, inside or outside; dense or lightweight; cloudy or foggy; mains or gas; acrylic or oil based. Machines are far superior to any homemade effects as they are so much more controllable. All machines should be safe to use however prolonged exposure to smoke can be uncomfortable for the eyes, nose and throat and notes should be made on the call sheet advising of its use.

Ambient temperature also has an affect on smoke, so bear in mind that that superb 'layered effect' seen first thing in the morning that the director loves, will be nigh on impossible to repeat when the set warms up later in the day!

When working outside it can be useful to have a self-powered lightweight machine and work upwind from the scene.

An Artem Exterior machine below, is ideal for this (other similar machines are available). These have a heating coil inside and run off gas and smoke canisters, sold usually on sale or return. When lit, the coil heats up and glows, then one releases the oil, turning into smoke as it flows through the coil. This is very controllable but at initial start up it tends to squirt out oil, so point away from valuables and people. Care must be taken to NOT tighten the control knobs excessively as these can occasionally strip their threads.

Artem Exterior Smoke Machine.

For interior use the Colt machines are very convenient and run for a while without a mains power connection. These provide a general smoke effect that dissipates quite quickly although it does produce quite a cloudy effect as opposed to a fog. These machines are very simple to operate and all come with instructions.

155

Colt 4 Smoke machine.

For an overall atmosphere and to create the impression of softness on film we used to have bee guns, they required lit charcoal sprinkled with incense all contained in a small hand held bellows. Now these should only be used outside and they have been superseded by the safer cracked oil machines, which trickle out smoke in a pulsing action. Prolonged use can still cause mild irritation though.

There are also other versions that provide a very similar effects like a cracked oil machine or the Rosco on the next page.

Rosco Fog Machine.

Alternative to machines.

It is possible to buy 'smoke pots' which are triggered by 9v batteries. These come in different colours and produce smoke over set time periods, however, once started, they have to fully run their course of time. Bear this in mind when the director shouts "cut".

Steam:

The most reliable method for creating steam on set must be a heavy duty steamer or a wallpaper stripper. Be aware though that it may not be visible if the set gets too hot. Smoke is often used as an alternative.

Wind:

As with smoke, there are various machines available. If working in remote areas a petrol machine is required, this tends to be quite large and requires it's own trailer. Only specialists should operate this type of machine.

Trailer Mounted machines, petrol and electric powered.

For more gentle interior scenes, floor-standing fans are the norm as below together with some more directional devices.

A Cinefex Fan, a Centrifugal Fan and a Makita hand blower.

Dry Ice:

Dry ice is a dense fog, which sinks to the floor. The material used is frozen Carbon Dioxide which is inherently dry and extremely cold (gloves required). When this is dipped into boiling water the ice creates a gas, expands and escapes wherever it can, usually through ducting supplied with a machine. There are two main versions of this machine, a Pea Souper and a Londoner. These machines are basically large 'kettles' with multiple kettle elements built inside a waterproof container.

Inside are hanging metal trays which, when loaded with ice, are lowered into the water, creating the effect. The 'Londoner' being a larger version with more elements and fans. They need to reach simmering temperature prior to use and they consume a lot of electricity. These can be dry hired and should come with ducting supplied.

The frozen CO_2 has to come from independent suppliers and is quite expensive. It can come in various forms but the best for these machines is 'pellets'. It's impossible to keep this material from heating up, so therefore if using large quantities a freezer is recommended for temporary storage (or, some cheap polystyrene fish boxes).

The machine hire company should be able to suggest the nearest CO_2 supplier but it is usually used near major airports where there should be a suppliers.

Pea Souper and Londoner dry ice machines above. Note: Gloves are required to avoid burns and the ice should not be transported with passengers in a vehicle.

Liquid Nitrogen:

This is even colder than dry ice and extreme caution is recommended. It can be ordered through any large pharmacy and comes in its own metal flask. Though a smoke is produced its main use is to fast freeze an item or to provide very low level 'pouring' smoke. Once dipped in the flask the item will freeze solid (if it contains any water) and will then break or smash if required. I once used this to provide an effect of a rose (flower) smashing on a floor for a dream sequence.

Water, Rain and Condensation:

Water effects on stages require special preparations. In fact it's often wise to choose a concrete as opposed to wooden stage floor if making a studio choice (see studios and tanks earlier in this book). Proper protection is necessary to avoid potential damage and cost, as water spills, if not dealt with will creep under a wooden floor making it expand and distort, thus requiring replacement. If creating any water effects make sure to have enough materials to build temporary floor trays where spillage can be collected and disposed of properly. A bag of sawdust can also be really useful to sprinkle and soak up small spills. You can guarantee this will happen at least at one hose connection!

Hot Water:

If building action pools, baths or showers, heating is necessary to keep the actors comfortable. It is possible to hire fully portable water heaters which consist of a header tank and portable gas heaters and it's wise to position these as close to the outlet taps as possible as the hot supply can rapidly cool if running over long distances on the floor. This may seem trivial but if an actor is adjusting the temperature for comfort it will not be consistent if the supply is some distance away and one can nearly fill a bath of cold water before it gets warm with long pipe runs. Drainage is also important often requiring the sets to be built on rostrums to allow for the waste water. If you are lucky some stages may have a floor drain, check in advance.

Rain:

Rain is rarely visible on camera unless extremely heavy, we generally only see the effects from the rain like puddles and on glass. These effects can generally be achieved with simple hose sprinkler systems bought at your local store or even spritzers. It is also possible to construct simple rain bars with drilled copper tube connected to a hose supply. If this is supported level and with the holes pointing upwards the rain should look fairly real, though it will fall in a straight line. Standard sprinklers are also useful for this but you will normally find that a minimum of two is required, one for background, or artist and one in foreground in front of the camera. A manifold is also advised to control front and background pressure levels. Snap-on hose connectors are very useful for the above effects.

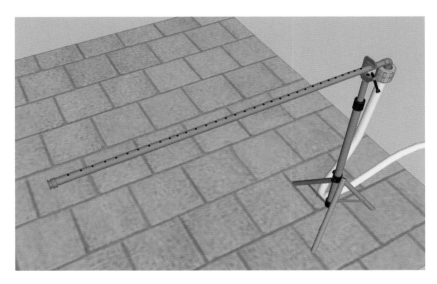

A Simple home made rain bar. Small regular holes drilled into a copper tube with a capped end, this needs to be set dead level, for a realistic effect.

The professional systems are obviously superior, with rotating bars dispersing the flow of water, all fixed to light stands. For much larger effects serious pressure is required with fire engine assistance or trucks using especially converted concrete pumps.

Wet Downs:

Multiple hoses are ideal for street wet downs as paving and tarmac tend to dry out remarkably quickly requiring constant attention, this can be frustrating for the director who may be dealing with multiple cues over a large area. It's worth locating a decent water source, or mobile bowser at the recce so as to secure your supply and have plenty of hose available, plus connectors and splitters. 3/4" hose is ideal for this but beware as you may need to get more connections quickly and local suppliers won't have them. Therefore I would recommend the smaller and more general 1/2" hoses, as the fittings are far easier to get at short notice.

Puddles:

Puddles present their own set of problems. They can be created easily in a natural hollow but this is rarely where one is required. There is no easy way to create these on location other than to take up paving slabs, create a hollow, line with heavy duty polythene and redress the paving slabs over (you will need permission from whoever owns the pavement here). Great care is required when re-dressing the slabs as it's easy to puncture the polythene. This can take time to create, and it's hard to get an exact camera angle about 4 shots in advance, so notify the assistant director to establish the exact position as early as possible, ideally on the recce. A small piece of glass or perspex could be temporarily laid down to establish a position and see the reflection.

Mist and Condensation on Glass:

As with many effects window condensation appears relatively straightforward to achieve simply with some steam on one side of glass. However, trying to achieve this with a camera kit and lights in close proximity can be fraught with problems. Eventually the steamer will have soaked everything around BUT the glass. The temperature fluctuates drastically with the lighting and all effects by natural means become virtually impossible. I would recommend using aerosol Anti Flare for condensation. This is like beeswax and can be sprayed carefully over the glass in varying degrees, it's relatively easy to clean off and lifelike shapes can be drawn on if required. There is usually a can of this right next to the camera crew.

When no anti-flare is available, similar effects can be created with spray glue or even wallpaper paste, though cleaning off is more difficult. For a permanent misted window, try frosted or even clear window film.

Snow, Ice and Frost:

Various different types of snow are available depending on the desired result, basically falling snow or settled snow, sometimes both. Special consideration should be taken regarding disposal once the job is complete and potential damage to wildlife and plants if working outdoors. Each product should be supplied with it's own data sheet explaining all hazards and this should be included on the call sheet. If in any doubt consult your special effects supplier.

We used to use dendritic salt, an agricultural product, however this is corrosive, especially when washed down drains.

Years ago I designed a complete arctic scene with this and our artist, a real polar bear, really liked the taste. This made him very thirsty, hence, drinking excessively, he soaked the set in polar bear urine!

Below is a list of the most commonly used materials to create snow on set, consult your supplier for further details and alternatives on each product.

Settled and Falling Snow:

Paper snow is probably the most economic for settled snow, available in fireproof and non-fireproof (the cheapest). The basic ingredient is mulched paper originally formulated for baby's nappies, as it's so absorbent. This is supposed to be harmless but does appear to cause irritation to nose and throat over long periods as it's incredibly dusty. If dressing a large area I would recommend spraying with water as it's laid, to keep the dust down, and using masks. The stuff also makes great snowballs, if mixed with water. When working over large areas and outside a Kendal type blower is used for dispersal.

163

Polymer powder is great if slippery snow under foot is required. This is mixed with water and expands up to 40 times it's own size. I remember dressing the floor of a complete set from just one bag out of my small van. Then returning half the bag back to the supplier unused! It is also good for mixing ever-lasting beer heads in commercial pack shots.

Snowcel paper settled snow.

This is ideal for most applications but can cause irritation and a dry throat if used over large areas.

Snowcel also comes in finer grades called:

'Half sized paper snow'.

Concept show falling snow.

This is used in Pacman snow rollers above the set. They are lightweight plastic flakes and being dry, can be used in many indoor locations or game shows. These machines look like fluorescent lights and hang above the set and can be loaded manually or automatically.

For falling snow on large areas a Snowboy water based system is the most popular, this ejects a dense foam which, when mixed with water and ejected falls slowly and realistically with adjustable flake size. This needs to be supplied with an operator.

Frost:

C90 Powder

This is a popular material for frost and light snow. Being relatively cheap it can be dressed virtually anywhere and it just washes away with rain or a hose. For small areas sprinkling through a sieve is recommended otherwise it can end up like lumpy flour. As this is relatively fine it can be very effective for models and close up. work.

For window frosting it is possible to buy aerosol sprays but the effect can be haphazard if not applied carefully.

Glistening Snow:

Magnesium Sulphate Crystals are the most professional solution, available from your snow effects supplier or pharmacy. Failing this, sugar is pretty effective.

Icicles:

These can be done in numerous ways with probably the most realistic being 'sugar glass' or resin. They can also be purchased in varying sizes on a vacuum formed clear sheet (good and cheap) but they require cutting out prior to hanging.

Pyrotechnics:

Anything involving gas, flames and explosions generally requires a qualified specialist and your shoot will not be insured if you try otherwise. This rule even applies to relatively simple tasks like using flame bars in a gas log fire. If filming outdoors in relative safety it is possible to buy and use certain effects, usually 9 volt battery operated smoke pots or bullet flashes (these require simple wiring up from a small battery to ignite). The specialist will recommend the crew required and should ensure all equipment is safe and will give you a price accordingly. If renting a mobile cooking unit the gas hose should be checked and a manufacturing date will be printed on it if from a reputable company. Note also that gas cookers will require different jets if natural gas is not used.

It's wise to check that fire extinguishers are at hand, either from the specialist or the studio, and that they have been tested, a 'last test' date will be on each extinguisher.

If planning a bigger effect, a large proportion of the cost will be in the preparation involved, as tests will need to be completed prior to the shoot. Hopefully these will be filmed so as everyone is clear what the effect will look like well before filming. A lot of this may seem over precautionary but this is one of the most dangerous jobs in the industry and there have been numerous accidents.

I had once to create an effect of a car being crushed under a concrete block. This eventually required six cars, colour matched, with engines removed and many other alterations. Three filmed tests were required on a special site and this just for the one effect. Even a fake concrete block had to be constructed so as to not damage the ground at the location.

Other simple looking effects requiring substantial prep are rigging bullet holes. This is done by pre drilling the holes, fitting charges, refilling and making good.

Do it yourself effects:

Some very effective shots can be completed without specialist contractors and these routes are definitely worth exploring at budget stage. Something as simple as a rock hitting a place on a wall will take considerable time if not thought about in advance and as we know, shoot time is money.

I once had to do a boulder smashing a model Parthenon. The boulder needed to hit the same spot six times before the shot looked right. If you can dictate exactly where the point of impact is you can be sure the camera will be framed and in focus saving valuable time. The same effect can be used for firing arrows into walls as seen in the following image:

If an arrow is pre-rigged on to a guide wire, it will always hit the target in the same place. This makes camera framing and focus easier.

On another occasion there was a request to drop all the props, at once, from an 'upside down set', as if they were being sucked up to the ceiling (when the picture was flipped). The obvious initial solution was to use electro magnets but this became unworkable with all the props being different weights. The problem was solved by fastening some u-shaped nylon threads to each of the props (as arrows above) then poking this through minute holes in the dressed desks and cabinets. On the reverse side of these, a nail was pushed through securing each item to its dressed position. When all the nails were fastened to one pull cord it would enable the props to all be released together with just one pull. No effects company, minimal materials and each take repeatable at minimal cost.

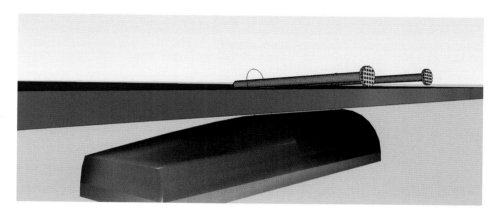

The Telephone above is hung to the ceiling with a nail release, pulled out on cue to drop the phone. This can be used with items of variable weights.

Another widely used effect is invisibly moving an object in close up.

Suppose an object is on a table top and needs gently moving across it. If one puts a piece of glass on the table, then places the object on that, the glass can be slid effectively moving the object invisibly. The addition of some small ball bearings from your local bike shop between the top and glass reduces friction.

If a fake crack is required in glass, it can be very easily achieved with a combination of both black and white 'Chinograph' wax pencils. The black looking like shadow and white being the highlight. This can look remarkably realistic especially when drawing on the tv screen or pane of glass.

On one past film I bought a new television under orders from the producer, in an attempt to reduce excessive hire fees. His intention was to take it from the truck after the three week Moroccan shoot to his home. Whilst awaiting the film crew we drew a fake crack on the screen as a joke just to see his reaction. With a quick wipe it was gone and we were ready for filming and much entertained.

A collapsing floor effect can be safely achieved with four upright supports, hinged in the centre, and pulled (at the hinges) on cue to drop the floor, see below.

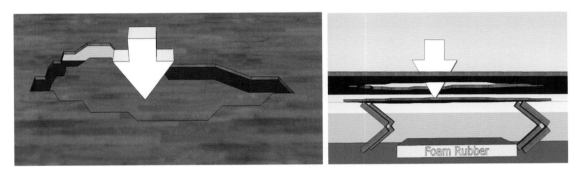

A safe collapsing floor effect using just hinges and foam rubber.

Collapsing floor effect seen on set above. The main problem is having enough space under the set, here the set is built over the stage tank.

Broken Glass:

Glass sheets and bottles are made using 'sugar glass' which is exactly that, glass made with sugar. This is very brittle and fragile so care is required during transport. It also is a slightly different colour so tends to be a bit yellow for close-up.

Other Simple DIY Effects:

There may be many obscure items asked for which have all been tried and tested for other productions so it's definitely worth an initial Internet search but here are a few of the most common ones (DO not inhale or ingest any of the following):

Effect required	Substitute	Notes
Blood	Olive Oil mixed with red, yellow or blue food colouring.	Mix a quantity into a sealable container before use to retain consistency.
Bullet hitting effects	Buy specially made runs and attach where required. Use small battery to detonate.	Must be over 18yrs to buy these from effects companies as per fireworks.
Candles	Use double wick candle for added brightness.	These burn quicker so check supply.
Champagne	Clear Ginger Beer or Fizzy Apple Juice.	Labelled and sealed bottles can be bought at prop houses.
Cobwebs	Aerosol fake cobwebs for close up or contact adhesive (UHU etc.).	Use sparingly, this can be hard to remove from valuables.
Cocaine	Menthol crystals from large Chemists.	Sniff only small quantities.
Condensation	Anti-Flare as used by camera crew.	Ask camera dept before borrowing.
Custard Pie Mix	Aerosol spray foam onto a pre-made base.	
Excrement	For toilet stains use barbeque sauce. With solids use melted chocolate/nuts.	Add oil for consistency.
Fake floating ice	Melt wax onto water or buy sugar glass.	See steam earlier in chapter.
Melting Snow	Grated Ice from above camera.	This melts perfectly on a surface.

Oil	Treacle.	Easier to clean up.
Red Wine	Red Grape juice.	Add Blackcurrant juice to make redder.
Smoke	Various methods.	See smoke earlier in this chapter.
Steam	Wallpaper stripper/steamer.	See steam earlier in this chapter.
Teardrops	Glycerine	Mix with water to alter consistency.
Medieval Burning torches	Paraffin in steel bucket, Old Stick, Rag, Fencing wire.	Tie rag to stick with wire. Dip into bucket then drain and light.
Vomit	Tinned vegetable soup mixed with tinned potato/leek soup.	Alter mix according to desired colour.
Whisky	Cola or similar.	Mix with water to dilute.
White Wine	White grape juice.	

One of the above effects was used on a commercial some time ago. A well known car oil company wanted to simulate oil pouring beautifully down the side of the tin in a visually accurate way. After much testing, model makers found that treacle was the best substitute as it poured so well and was the most accurate colour and texture. The model makers then made up a pallet load of specially labeled gallon tins and had them delivered early to the studio ready for filming. Unfortunately, the studio was not yet open so they were left near the entrance door to the big stage and were stolen. This was not necessarily surprising as surrounding the studio were about six car garages all specializing in exotic cars. I wonder how many cars had their oil changed for treacle!

Summarizing, many effects can be achieved with a little foresight and lateral thinking. A considerable amount of money can be saved keeping things simple by using everyday items in a different and imaginative way. These effects can often be superior as they sometimes add a little inconsistency and reality rather than relying on the post-production solutions we see so often. A competent prop man should carry a variety of application and mixing tools for the entire previous list but I have also found keeping a selection of syringes, measuring bowls and kitchen basters at home particularly useful.

GRAPHICS

 A specialist department usually deals with the graphics on feature films. Any practical computers or televisions on set generally need something on screen and this requires careful planning and budgeting early in the production. Photos of the cast, possibly as children, may be needed for set dressing, or newspaper articles. Period productions require extensive research for all the dressing props etc. A special column should be created in the feature film breakdown to list as many graphics as possible from the script, others will be sure to follow.

On smaller productions like commercials and shorts it may be possible to delegate this job to a loyal assistant, or even take the task on yourself. Many elements can be created on a home computer, although we are often restricted to the output size of our home printer and scanner. This can include things like product labels or static on-screen computer images. There are many companies who specialize in this, but it is the art director who often has to create initial artwork or prepare a brief.

Copyright:

Always remember the basic copyright laws, especially when using images taken off the Internet for your production. These laws are especially critical on commercials where buy out fees, can be prohibitive, as commercials are so widely seen. Remember, if you've created it, you own the copyright, but using others' work can be lead to problems. Finding out too late can be extremely expensive and jeopardize your relationship with your employer.

Computer On-screen Images:

Not being a specialist I have reservations about getting computers up and running on shoots. It may be relatively straightforward creating the initial graphic for your home computer screen, but loading this onto a rented computer monitor, in front of an impatient assistant director, to look correct on screen can shorten your life -especially if you are at all unsure about the monitor settings! So I would strongly advise getting a specialist to do this. Usually they can rent you the kit as well to keep within budget and do it for a fixed price. When doing it oneself, the simplest method I have found is to create a jpeg the correct size (as the final screen resolution), then install this as a screensaver on the action computer. This can then be set to run automatically after a few seconds.

Vinyl lettering:

As part of designing the set it's possible to create the signage artwork. Adobe Illustrator is the ideal software for this as it produces clear vector based images but we aren't all familiar with this software. As a result, Corel Draw or Photoshop will suffice but if creating text it's advisable to save it as separate layers so that the sign writer can manipulate the text easily, separate from the background colour when the letters are machine cut. If one does send standard 'flattened' jpeg artwork remember to only apply a dimension in one direction, ie; length OR height (not both) as text spacing can be different on different systems and your jpeg may differ a little in scale, compared with what they create at the printers.

When applying vinyl signs, temporarily place onto the surface prior to sticking. Then mark a horizontal line across the base of all the letters (on the backing paper) and once centred, mark the edges. Take it down and peel back just one corner of the sticky side, spritz the window (if glass) with a soap and water solution, then place into position again and gradually peel back the remaining backing paper. Once removed the lettering can be slightly manipulated then squeegeed down to remove all the bubbles. I've also found using low tack vinyl helpful to ease removal but if only high tack is available, it should still be removable after a day. Any longer one should rub petroleum jelly on the original surface to aid removal prior to fixing.

Take care also to check the artwork prior to fixing. I was once caught out when having a large clock face created to hang above the car for a Renault commercial. The roman numerals, seen as reflections in the windscreen and the bonnet, were by error created flipped and no one on the shoot noticed. The first person to realize this was the editor whilst cutting the final film, leading to some unexpected retouching costs!

Logos, Packs and Printed Images:

All these graphics require a working knowledge of the right software, namely Adobe Illustator and Photoshop. If one is familiar with this software, it's especially useful to keep a small backup supply of spare printer inks, glossy card, transparent paper, and even transfer material at home as creating these images is so often done in the evening after work when the shops are shut. Doing this work requires concentration on the computer and the stage production office with almost constant calls and interruptions is far from ideal. Another useful tip is to print one or two pixel border around your work, which aids the cutting and trimming consistency when you are in a hurry, this can then easily be done by an assistant on the shoot the following day. Remember also that unlike in professional printing, domestic ink is not waterproof, so sealing your final printed work with fixative or acrylic sealer will make it more resilient as your print can then be wiped clean easily if required. Always test a sample prior to sealing as the colours may change. Your materials expense should be reimbursed or at least replaced so you remain prepared for the next production.

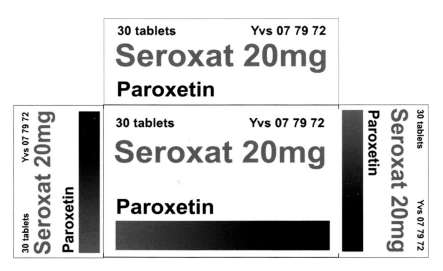

This pack was created for a programme about teenage depression where the manufacturers name required removing plus any bar codes. Putting a thin black cutting line around your work can aid the cutting out. I had initially sourced a compatable box, and then resized the artwork to fit easily on top.

Fake Money:

We are quite frequently asked to supply bank notes for productions and, as you may be aware, it is illegal to reproduce any currency. In fact, most scanners have built-in software to prevent this, as I once discovered this to my surprise. This problem can usually be overcome either by asking permission from your country's bank and supplying suitable artwork for approval (they have set conditions for duplicating fakes), or easier, trying to rent notes from existing prop houses. Getting permission can take up to two weeks. Having your own artwork created can be expensive as notes are designed to be complicated. However one can get away with remarkable inaccuracies if seen in the right context. Just try to avoid using both real and fake in the same take!

Fake currency artwork should be pre approved from your country's bank by law prior to printing, as there are special conditions to be met.

WORKING IN FOREIGN COUNTRIES

 Filming abroad can present its own set of difficulties because of language and different working practices, and as art directors we are often separated from the rest of the unit so translation can be problematic. Materials readily available at your base can be often difficult to source or even describe to local workers when substitutes may be available. *I remember once shipping 4 cwt of fuller's earth from the UK to southern Spain only to find it readily available and quarried locally 3 km away from the unit base.*

Specialist materials like gauze, paint stainers and effects materials are generally absent from most translation books and almost impossible to describe through local interpreters. Many of these may be sourced from mainland Europe or the Americas so it may be worth taking some small samples from your base if at all possible. These can then be physically shown as opposed to verbally described.

Dimensions from your elevations should also be in the local units, as these are usually done prior to travel. Also take all original relevant computer files with you for future editing if required.

179

A 'Pay as you go' dongle is a worthwhile (local) purchase as hotel Internet services can be expensive especially if staying for long periods, and a plug in mouse for your laptop or even a pen and tablet if creating visuals. Other essentials are a camera memory card reader and of course electrical adaptors.

Paint colours are often difficult to pin down as the 'Pantone' colour chart, although international, is not very practical when defining paint (as it's designed for printers ink) and colour charts tend to be standard to the local manufacturers only. A colour on a computer monitor is backlit and dependent on the monitor settings so cannot be relied upon. There is no easy remedy here other than picking up a local colour chart whilst recce-ing prior to the job. I remember once relating to a pack of chewing gum, internationally sold, to select a tone of blue for our sky backing in Prague.

Prop houses tend to be less frequent around Europe so hiring or buying has to be done through shops, which often operate different opening hours, although they do appear more accommodating when one wants to return the goods. Prop selection takes longer as a result and the art director usually has to accompany the prop buyer to be assured of the correct selection.

In general though I have found the crews tend to be very adaptable and keen to help out despite the extremely long hours and all the departments gel together very well considering the language difficulties.

There are of course many occasions where peoples experience must not be taken for granted. I once remember showing a local Moroccan driver a short length of timber and requesting about 200m of it from the local supplier as our standby supplies were depleted. On his return from the 3hr round trip through the desert I was surprised not to see this strapped to his Land Rover roof rack as he seemed to understand my request very well. Upon opening the back door, he had had it pre cut into two hundred one metre lengths making it useless for my needs!

Construction methods differ between countries. In this set built in Prague, the walls are built from chipboard, as opposed to plywood, requiring substantial bracing due to the extra weight.

HEALTH AND SAFETY

 The law varies from country to country but a designer is responsible for the safety and structural integrity of the design at all stages of its construction. You should also ensure that the materials involved are safe to use and notify the producer of any concerns you may have, including working excessive hours. Your crew should be competent for the tasks they are required to undertake. A more exhaustive list can be found with your local government health and safety department and it is mandatory that this is observed and followed.

There has only one instance of me having to re-build a set section because of safety concerns and this was on a commercial in Prague involving a large staircase being used for dancers to enter the scene. The structure was high and not built in the usual way, as a consequence it moved separately from the handrail and this, in my opinion, was not safe. All was sorted without question from the construction manager.

The main issues worth serious consideration are:

Is The Set Safe:

All walls and stairs and rostra need to be securely fixed to a supporting floor or rig especially hanging structures. The construction manager should comply with this but if you have any doubts, question and test it as any incident will involve all responsible.

Glass:

This is often used in scenery and regulations need following regarding the type of glass allowed for specific jobs. As a precaution glass should be taped to make visible whenever it is possible to walk into it.

Fire Risk:

All materials used should have been tested and have a recent fire risk certificate. These certificates are readily available from the suppliers and are measured in heat and flame resistance (half an hour, 1 hour etc.) for a fire to penetrate the surface and take hold. It often depends where your scenery is being used that determines the risk factor so final assembly in say a live event like a show, would be higher than a film stage, as the general public are involved. Simply painting the scenery or coating it in a flameproof liquid can accomplish much of this prevention. Also keeping all fire-ways and exits clear from materials and scenery and props.

Working at heights:

Ensuring handrails and other safety measures are included on any accessible structure and that areas of danger are clearly marked such as water tanks or holes in the floor. Any suspended items should have safety lines to prevent falling should any fastenings fail. The old rules used to specify a maximum height of six feet before mandatory handrails should be applied to the risers but the new rules are less specific, requiring **any** height, which could be at risk of trip or falling, should have sufficient safety measures. Expert advice should be sought when constructing all platforms including audience seating and lifting platforms.

Note also that any mechanical riser (scissor lift/ cherry picker/ fork lift etc.) requires certificates of competence for the operator.

Power tools and plant hire:

Ensuring operators are suitably qualified and competent. Individuals in control of tools, machinery and other work equipment have legal responsibilities for their safe operation.

Electrical Safety:

All electrical equipment and props should be safe to use and be recently PAT tested by a qualified electrician.

Gas Safety:

All portable gas equipment should be supplied on set in a safe and working condition (this means don't bring it from a friend unless he has the required safety certificates). All professional suppliers should have this information at hand. There are further regulations requiring especially trained technicians to deal with any naked flames on set and this may involve employing a specialist just to do this task. If supplying any portable gas bottles the hosing and regulators must be date stamped and comply to the current regulations.

Location:

All filming and build areas should be assessed for overall safety especially if working at night and preventative measures made prior to work commencement. This should include adequate lighting on the strike.

The previous list is by no means comprehensive but I have sadly witnessed many unexpected accidents, which could all have been avoided. Unfortunately I don't think excessive working hours are considered seriously enough in our industry and this risk is often overlooked and abused especially if one includes the commute to and from your place of work in hours overall. Accidents tend to be more frequent when crews are tired and it's late at night. By law we are required to rest breaks of at least 11hrs, weekly breaks of at least 35 hours or a fortnightly break of at least 59hrs. This is the law, and should not be abused despite budget issues. It is also an 'option' for anyone to do overtime rather than an 'obligation'.

A designer is responsible for completing a full risk assessment for each production and should highlight any potential areas of risk. A construction manager has similar obligations should he be contracted. A qualified first aider or unit nurse should be present on all shoots and they should also be there for the wrap (often late at night) to insure adequate safety measures are taken. Finally all the above hazards should be identified on the call sheet prior to commencement of the shoot.

Many accidents can be easily avoided with simple common sense and regular assessment, like wearing the right shoes or protective glasses etc. It's wise to always carry an art dept first aid kit and fire extinguisher as an addition to the production or studios' own as we are often working in different areas, with different risks. If working, please remember that a health and safety risk assessment will be required and in accordance with the law of each country. Extra vigilance is required with action vehicles and special effects where fuel may be present and insurance clarification is sometimes nescessary.

IF IT CAN, IT WILL

 As a final chapter I thought I'd include some of the more interesting times in my career in the film industry, which, though far from amusing at the time, provided much topical conversation after the event. Trust me, all were true.

I was introduced at quite a young age to professional art direction. At a time when the quality music video industry was in it's infancy. A new and exciting era, to which my services became much in demand. The financial rewards were far less than the life experiences though and many of the jobs were done on a shoestring budget demanding of both the director and designer.

There was one memorable time being asked to design two pop promos being filmed over two weeks in the Caribbean, the deal was one hundred pounds fee per week. I remember a day prior to traveling getting messages from the director, still writing his treatment, requesting certain props from the UK prior to the shoot. One of the items was for potential smoke effects. Being slightly naive, I decided to buy six white smoke pots, and put them in my suitcase.

The effects were never used on the shoot and remained in my empty suitcase throughout the week. In fact it wasn't until the last evening that their presence became an issue at all. This was when we were returning from a nightclub, post shoot, in our crew hire van. A local police force had set up a routine roadblock in an attempt to curb the drug dealing, just outside the town, and being a van containing six blokes late at night, we were soon stopped and searched. One of the officers asked what was in the suitcases to which the reply was "all empty". I'd completely forgotten about the smoke, the pots were grey in colour with a transparent lid containing thin red and black wires. When one connects these to a small battery it detonates the smoke and to the uninitiated they look remarkably like bombs. The Police, of course, decided to check inside the one case containing these and before long we were all lined up facing loaded guns. It was a long night proclaiming our innocence and I was not the most popular among the crew following our arrest! After three hours interrogation that night we were summoned to return again the following day. As we were also flying home we all decided to do a runner instead to the airport and left the pots, with the case at the police station.

Continuing on the police theme one of my first film production jobs as an art dept assistant was on a film production in remote mainland Greece. Packing for just a week I ended up staying the full course of this seven-week shoot as they were so short handed. The locals were unhappy about their remuneration mid shoot and planned to strike the following day (their idea of striking was to stand in front of the camera!) but being as we had inside information we filmed from a second camera at a different location. It wasn't long before we were all arrested for not having the correct work permits (any excuse), and we were all trundled off to the police station. The local town was a refreshing change for us as we hadn't seen much civilized habitation for quite some time but we were stuck in this very small station with just one officer, who could barely type, trying to process endless permit documents for the twenty of us. Eventually we decided to take things into our own hands. Our prop man took over the typing, while our interpreter dictated and our new work permits were done in record time much to the annoyance of the overwhelmed policeman. Back to work in five hours after a trip round the town!

On this same film I remember recceing for a derelict church in this rather desolate area. We were confident of finding the ideal location and sure enough, nestling in the valley less than an hour away was this tatty looking small village hall. The paint was flaking and the building beautifully rust stained yet sun bleached, even the owners were accommodating around our tight six-week shoot schedule. Unbeknown to us the owners were so thrilled of their building featuring in our film that they had it entirely re-rendered and whitewashed, exactly two days prior to filming. The next day saw me ageing it back down to how it was in the first place!

On another amusing occasion I was working on a Feature film in Dartmoor, England. The script required that all leading actors be made to look as though they were in an extreme 'drugs orgy'. That night in my hotel bedroom I was preparing the prop drugs for the next days shoot. This involved delicately measuring out menthol, a safe and suitable substitute for cocaine. Cutting it up with a blade and putting it into my pre-cut wrappers made from foil, enough for 20 people. As this was time consuming, I had pre-ordered my supper and had it sent to my room for the evening's work. The look of astonishment on the chambermaid's face was delightful when the meal arrived at my door seeing my concoction and the hotel staff appeared genuinely wary of me for the next following few weeks' stay!

Then there are the sets that went up and came down, without any filming being done. A return flight to Los Angeles, a 25 thousand dollar set on a large stage in LA and a phone call to ask how much it would cost to take it down on our last days build! This all because of a certain recording artist overstaying her time in rehab. I had to return three months later for the set rebuild at major cost to them.

I once designed and had built a large split level office with a glass wall overlooking a well-known football stadium for a telecoms advertisement. The star, a football manager, due to a misunderstanding with his agent failed to show up resulting in the set coming down, going into storage and being re-built a week later in a different stage. A welcome cancellation fee for all concerned.

They say never work with kids and animals. A stylish hi-fi commercial utilising the black and white 'bar codes' used in retail was the theme for my next tale. One scene was supposed to show a flock of especially dyed black birds flying out from behind black boards that were set against a striped background, this representing a huge bar code. Two rods supported the small black panels used to hide the birds before flight. One being the perch and one the support for the board, a third rod being used to prod the bird from behind and make them fly away. It so happens the birds didn't want to fly that morning and preferred to merely shuffle along to the end of the rod despite all our prodding. The short lunch saw me swapping all the rods around in an effort to succeed. With the support rod moved to the top, the perch could be pulled out from under them, the birds would have to fly, I thought. No such luck, with just the camera crew and clients remaining on the viewer side of the set, as the rest of us were behind the set nurturing birds. All we heard was laughter as 20 birds were seen falling onto the floor in complete disarray. Fortunately it was the birds that got replaced as opposed to the art director.

Here I also learned how to catch escaped birds stuck up in the studio rig. Just light a candle on the stage floor and turn the house lights out. Eventually all the birds would fly down to the candlelight where they can be carefully caught and put away never to be seen on that stage ever again!

Summarising, after all my years working in the film industry, the best advice I can provide is that every shoot is another steep learning curve!

ACKNOWLEDGEMENTS

 Special thanks to Rick at Artem Special Effects for permission to use their photos (taken by Bob Thorn) and also Nick Pearce, scenic painter, who assisted in the paint effects and advice. The paint samples section could not have been completed without the help of Callum and Rigby Andrews of Halliford Studios UK who loaned their studios, lighting and workshop facilities throughout. A big thankyou of course to the many directors and other clients without whom, there would be no information or photos!

My two sons Matthew and Lester who are still freshers in the demanding film careers they have chosen together with their mother Jill without whom this book would still be a seedling in my imagination. My friend Sonia Adams who helped me persevere through the trials and traumas of actually writing it. A mention must also go to the present and past students of UCCA Farnham film production who helped me define what I thought needed writing.

My father Ken worked as a scenic artist and in an attempt to supplement his earnings he often worked late into the night 'moonlighting' on tv commercial sets. On one occasion whilst still very young I accompanied him onto a western 'cowboy' scene in a small studio in Barnes, London, where he was touching up his sky backing. As they were recording sound, crushed cork was used underfoot to simulate the loose gravel chippings and all within a fantastically accurate outdoor American scene. It all looked so real, yet was scenery and I was smitten. It was here I realized my ambition.

After my father left the RAF, he worked in carpentry, general building and theatre design. This led to working for the BBC where he, Tony Common and Eric Critchley developed new methods in scenic painting. This often involved using the dark shadow colours to prime their backings, as opposed to the then standard white paint. They named their specially mixed 'Redaluma' colours 'Shepherds Bush Green' and 'Shepherds Bush Brown'. Using this new method they then only needed to paint where the light touched, and left the rest to go into shadow, which saved time yet looked more effective as well. They cut foam paint rollers into leaf and stone shapes, even brick, to reproduce quick repeat patterns. This transformed the way backings were painted and this system was soon used universally throughout this specialised trade.

Eventually he formed Westbridge Studios in London with my two brothers Mark, Simon and myself. My mother Nina, already an accomplished artist, often painted the backdrops. Ken, using his remarkable painting and building abilities moved seamlessly into set design. This was in a period when good film directors were seen as the solution to a successful advertising campaign, and budgets took on a lesser role. Today the reverse is prevalent, and much of the industry has changed. Ken was relentless in his job, working tirelessly to achieve perfection. He was my mentor. Throughout his life he supported me both emotionally and many times financially, and I learnt an enormous amount from his actions and words. I also learnt about creative people, whether chippies, painters or clients- all often eccentric in their ways. He encouraged and helped on many of my earlier set designs giving me that all-important 'first step' on the ladder of an art director. He was proud when eventually I took on some of his clients as well, and I never looked back.

This book I dedicate to Ken Hill 1922-2010.

GLOSSARY

Action Vehicle- *Vehicle specifically chosen to appear on screen.*

3D Printer- *A machine capable of creating three-dimensional shapes direct from plans.*

Animatronics- *The use of electronics and mechanics to assist in the movement of puppets.*

Apprenticeships- *People employed specifically to learn on the job.*

Art Department- *The specific people working on props, scenery, wardrobe and makeup.*

Atmospherics- *Specialist in air, clouds, gasses, smoke and moisture to form weather.*

Backcloth- *A cloth (usually canvas) hung to act as a background to the set.*

Background Artists- *People who support the main actors used often in the background.*

Blacklist- People or companies with a poor record of payments from past contracts.

Brief- *Explanation of job prior to implementation.*

Budget- *List of expected expenditure on a specific project.*

Budget Breakdown- *List as above with separate areas for specific tasks, transport and materials.*

Button Polish- *A form of shellac varnish (see 'shellac').*

Cable Tie- *A quick disposable fastening usually made from plastic.*

Calcium carbonate- *A whitish aggregate commonly known as 'Lime'.*

Call-sheet (contact sheet)- *A list of all key crew on a production together with contact details.*

Celluloid- *The material camera film is made of.*

Chain Tackle- *A geared winch system either mechanically or electrically operated.*

Checking off (props)- *A method quantifying props on arrival and return.*

Cherry Picker- *A mobile crane with an Arial platform capable of supporting a work-man.*

Chroma key- *A colour often used in film or video for compositing two images together.*

Cladding- *A surface applied to cover an interior structure.*

Clapperboard- *A special board used to record film takes and synchronize the sound and image.*

Client- *The potential buyer of your services.*

Cloudbuster- *A device created by Willhelm Reich (1950's) using orgone energy to create clouds.*

CNC- *Computer numerical control. A system devised for modeling/cutting using a computer.*

Colour Chart- *A paint manufacturer's chart showing available colours in their range.*

Concept Sketch- *A sketch drawn quickly to describe something as a discussion aid.*

Continuity- *The consistency of characters, events, location or objects as seen earlier in the same production.*

Counterweight- *An equivalent counterbalancing weight to support a hanging load.*

Cyc, cyclorama- *A background created to seamlessly merge the floor with the walls.*

Dolly- *A device designed to carry the camera and manoeuver it smoothly in all directions.*

Dongle- *A small piece of computer hardware created to enable remote internet connection.*

DOP- *Director of photography, controls the light exposure and often operates the camera.*

Dressing (set)- *Furnishing a set with furniture and props.*

Dry Hired- *Can be hired on its own without an operator.*

Estimate (cost)- *A realistic guess as to how much a job will cost based on previous experience.*

Ezy-Up- *A trade name for a mobile canopy easily erected and dismantled.*

Fast-Cast- *A two-part material that sets when mixed and put in a mould.*

Flat- *A re-usable piece of scenery often used to create walls in sets.*

Flattage- *A group of flats fastened together.*

Float- *Scenery designed to move or an amount of money lent to a contractor.*

Frame- *A single frame of film in a movie camera.*

Frame number- *Frames as above, are numbered for ease of recording and editing.*

Freeholder- *The owner of a property.*

Gaffer- *The head of the electrical department.*

Gauze- *A thin transparent fabric made from cotton, similar to a net but with a fine weave.*

Generator- *A portable engine designed to create electricity.*

Graphics- *Artwork created for packages, presentation and video etc.*

Grow-lights- *Special ultra violet lights to assist plant growth.*

Hard Drive- *A digital device for recording data in a computer system.*

Hierarchy- *An arrangement of items in a specific order.*

Initial Script- *A script suitable for adjustment after review.*

Lichen- *A fungus that often grows on rocks.*

Kays Art Department- *A film production manual used to locate facilities, crew and equipment.*

Locking Off- *A camera position where the camera should not be moved or adjusted.*

Logging- *A system for manually recording film or video takes.*

Logistics- *Managing flow from the point of origin to the point of use.*

Low Resolution- *Digital images, the higher the resolution the greater the detail in the image.*

Magazine (film)- *A lightproof container used to load film into cameras.*

Mark-up- *A percentage added to the overall total to cover expenses and profit.*

Memory card- *A removable device for recording data specific to a camera or electronic device.*

Meths- *Short for Methylated Spirits.*

Mood Board- *A display to describe the overall style of a design or film set.*

Motion Control- *A computerized rig capable of pre-programming for repeat camera moves.*

Mouldings- *Created in marble, plaster and wood to be used as a decorative feature in rooms.*

Movement order- *Written directions created to find locations.*

PA- *A personal assistant.*

Pack shot- *A shot of the product in a commercial.*

Pad (wooden)- *A piece of packing, usually wood to screw into and provide support.*

PAT test- *Portable appliance test, for electrical appliances.*

PDF- *Portable document format. An open standard for document exchange.*

Photoshop- *Computer software created by Adobe systems for image manipulation.*

Plywood- *A type of timber where multiple sheets are glued together to form a single sheet.*

Polystyrene- *A kind of expanded foam used for sculpting and moulding shapes.*

Polythene- *Plastic waterproof sheeting sometimes known as 'viscuine'.*

Post Production- *A process used to complete a film once shooting is complete.*

Preformatted Budget- *A template created to complete budgets on.*

Production Company (film)- *A company that specializes in filmmaking.*

Production Designer- *Person responsible for the overall look of the film.*

Props- *Objects used in film or theatre, short for properties.*

Pyrotechnics- *The science of working with explosives and chemicals.*

Quote (budget)- *A price that someone, or company is willing to complete a project for.*

Recce- *A pre-shoot reconnaissance of a film location.*

Reference- *An image or item used to refer to when creating designs or items.*

Rheostat- *A device used to reduce or increase electrical current.*

Rig (film)- *A system used for fixing or hanging an item.*

Rostrum- *A temporary platform or stage.*

Rsj- *A rolled steel joist or 'I' beam primarily used to support heavy structures.*

Sat Nav- *Abbreviation for satellite navigation system to aid direction finding.*

Scaffolding- *A method of using tubular steel or alloy and clamps to build, support or work from.*

Scenery- *A temporary structure used in film or theatre production.*

Scumble- *A special slower drying clear glaze used for creating paint effects.*

Set Design- *A design for scenery usually showing the finished look with elevations and plans.*

Shellac- *Flakes derived from insects which, when dissolved in alcohol makes a liquid suitable for sealing surfaces.*

Shoot (film)- *The actual process of making a film.*

Shoot schedule- *A breakdown of the process created prior to making a film in an efficient way.*

Show reel- *A selection of videos done by an individual to showcase his/her work.*

Sketch-up- *A 3D computer software program created by Google to aid design.*

Squeegee- *A tool to aid removal of bubbles and wrinkles from vinyl.*

Stage- *A platform or presentation area for actors and shows.*

Storyboard- *A selection of images created in sequential order to describe the shots in a film.*

Strike (set)- *The process of dismantling the scenery at the end of production.*

Studio- *A specifically designed area for presentation of shows, events and performances.*

Subcontractor- *People working and paid for by a main contractor.*

Sugar Glass- *Specially created using sugar to make breakable glass designed to shatter.*

Take (film, video)- *The part of a movie between editing points in the final film.*

Tarpaulin- *A sheet of strong flexible and waterproof material used for protecting items.*

Tech Recce- *As recce above but with all heads of department present.*

The Knowledge- *A film production manual to locate facilities, crew and equipment.*

Track (camera)- *A portable track assembled to aid the smooth movement of the camera.*

Tracking Boards- *Special boards used to lay the camera tracks on.*

Trestle Table- *A collapsible and portable worktable.*

Wardrobe Rail- *Portable tubular framework for hanging and storage of clothes.*

Weft- *Cross-threads woven into the material.*